WELLNESS WISDOM

Little Book of Wellbeing

by

LU LAW

ISBN (eBook): 979-8-89604-794-0

ISBN (Paperback): 979-8-89604-795-7

ISBN (Hardback): 979-8-89604-796-4

Table of Contents

Introduction

Writing the Book I Needed to Read

There is a simple truth I have come to learn on my long journey of healing: we always write the books we need to read. We speak the words we most need to hear. This book, in its very essence, is a collection of the lessons, truths, and gentle reminders I needed to gather to save myself. It is, first and foremost, a testament to the wisdom I fought so hard to learn. It is a legacy for my children and granddaughter, who are my greatest teachers. It is the map I wish I'd had, and it is the wisdom I hope to pass on to them. I have written it for my readers who may come across it at precisely the moment it is needed.

My Story

My journey begins in a beautiful little village in the Spanish Pyrenees. As a child, I would watch planes flying across the blue sky, imagining that one day I would be on one of them, leaving the village and travelling across the globe. That opportunity came after university, when a friend suggested going to London. There, I met my husband, and my fate changed forever.

I became so busy building a family and pursuing a 25-year career in teaching that wellness was never a consideration. For years, I felt powerless in my own body, suffering from debilitating period pains and hormonal imbalances that doctors could not explain. These pains were so severe that I could neither walk straight nor breathe easily.

At age forty, I realised a fundamental truth: without your health, you cannot enjoy anything else. As the saying goes, health is not everything, but without it, everything is nothing. My journey to wellness began not with gentle curiosity, but with a desperate need.

The Purpose of This Book

The pages that follow are the culmination of a twenty-year quest. It is designed to help you **avoid prolonged struggle.** Do not take twenty years to learn some of the things I write in this book! Unlike me, who spent a lifetime searching externally, perhaps it is time to take a U-turn and look inside ourselves for solutions.

I wrote this book for one simple reason: so that your journey need not be as long or as painful as mine. One thing

I know for sure: if we do not make time for wellness, we will be forced to make time for illness.

Who This Book Is For?

In my heart, I have written this book for two kinds of women:

- **The Younger Woman:** So she can see what is around the corner before she gets there, armed with the wisdom to navigate her life with more grace and fewer hard lessons.
- **The Older Woman:** For those who have slogged through raising a family, pursuing a career, and caring for ageing parents. For the woman who, after a lifetime of putting everyone else first, is finally realising that this is her time.

This book is your permission slip to put yourself first, to make yourself the main project in your life, and to start making every single day count. Whether we acknowledge it or not, we are all on a countdown, and the time to live fully is now.

For my students, this book is definitely for you if I have taught you in the last twenty-five years!

About the Book

This is not a book of quick fixes, but a fast track to wellness drawn from my own experience. My friend, the writer Carmen Harris, is part of a group of us, nutritionists, healers, and yoga teachers, who meet regularly. We call ourselves the "Nymphs of North London." Each of us cooks something healthy and gathers to share food, knowledge, and inspiration. During one of our lunches, Carmen coined the term "wellness junkies," which I have happily embraced.

In a world where many are addicted to things that numb them, being addicted to wellness is a wonderful pursuit. It is a beautiful obsession to constantly seek conditions that allow you to feel in control of your life and health. In a world of addictions, choosing a beneficial one is a powerful act.

Sharing My Knowledge

For years, friends and colleagues encouraged me to share my knowledge, but I was reluctant. Last year, I studied Astrology with the wonderful Debra Silverman. She taught us that our North Node represents our life's mission, the reason we are here. Mine is in Leo, which means: *"I have come here to enthuse, inspire, and shine."* Even though these qualities do not always come naturally to my introverted heart, I knew I had to feel the fear and do it anyway.

While writing this book, I encountered many people with the intention of writing a book. In fact, I believe we all have a book or a film inside us, but to actually execute it is a completely different matter. When I attended the Hays House writer's workshop, we were told, *"If you write, you are a writer."*

This is my encouragement for all of you: if I can do it, so can you.

This book is my act of courage. It is me stepping into my purpose. If, after reading, you feel called to continue this journey with more personal guidance, I welcome you to connect with me at **luciaalaw@gmail.com**.

A Choice for Later Life

As we age, we are presented with a clear choice. Some of us spend our later years going from one doctor's appointment to the next, our lives dictated by illness. This is a staggering 50 percent of people over 50 who suffer from a chronic condition, spending many years in pain and relying on medication. Others from among us follow a different path, by prioritising our well-being at relatively younger stages of life so we can enjoy those same years full of vitality, freedom, and joy.

The real luxuries in life are not possessions, but what we feel:

- A calm nervous system
- Strong gut health
- Great energy
- Time with loved ones
- Quality sleep

Life is precious and fleeting. It is too short to be lived in pain or stress. Let us make the time we have the best it can possibly be.

The journey starts here, no matter where you are in life. From my soul to yours, welcome!

How to Use This Book

This book is an invitation to embark on a gentle and profound journey back to yourself. It can be read as a normal book, but if you really want to deeply benefit from it, this book can be used as a companion for when you need some inspiration to help you transform. If you are struggling with a certain area in your life, you can go to the relevant section and read what might help you or remind you what you could do.

To receive the maximum benefit from our time together, I encourage you to approach it not as a race, but as a slow, mindful pilgrimage.

Please, read this book slowly

In a world that is constantly throwing information at us, our capacity to absorb and integrate wisdom has become strained. This is not a book to be devoured in a single weekend. Instead, I invite you to read one chapter at a time. After each one, pause. Give yourself the gift of time, which is one of the most precious things we have.

At the end of every chapter, you will find two invitations for practice: **Your Wisdom to Go**, which offers simple, actionable steps to try during your week, and **Your Journal Prompts**, which are designed for deeper, quieter reflection. Please, do not skip these sections. They are where the true magic happens. This is where the ideas move from the page and into the fabric of your life. Also journaling is the cheapest form of therapy!

Treat this book as a loving companion. It is meant to be read and re-read. The truth is, we know everything that is in this book. This wisdom resides within all of us. But we forget. Even though I have written the book myself, I forget the ideas that are in it. In the process of editing the book, which has taken me over four years to write, I have reminded myself of many of the ideas. It is because even though we know, we need reminding. I believe that we teach what we need to learn, and when we do it, we consolidate our knowledge. My greatest hope is that these chapters will serve as a beautiful and powerful reminder of the wisdom you already hold within.

When I started the journey, I did a Louise Hays course and the facilitator asked us what we wanted to achieve. After thinking long and hard, I decided that I wanted inner peace. In order to live with inner peace, it is important not to hate anyone (including politicians, which seems to be a challenge for all of us at the moment), not compare ourselves to others, not worry about the past or the future, not to expect to get what we give, and not to complain about difficulties.

One thing I know for sure, if we do not make time for wellness, we will be forced to make time for illness. When I lost my two brothers at age 53 and 63, out of the great despair I felt, I decided that I needed to learn the art of living. On the way, I have learnt to look after myself to live well and not live to look after myself and also to be flexible and open to new information.

It is a fact that chronic illness is crippling the economy and making drug manufacturers very rich. One in ten people around the world live with an autoimmune disease. I read that one in two people in United Kingdom will be diagnosed with cancer. Maybe our journey here is not about becoming anything but more about unbecoming everything that is not really us so that we can be who we were meant to be in the first place.

Do not take twenty years to learn some of the things I write in the book! Unlike me who has been searching out there all my life, maybe it is also time to take a U-turn and

look inside ourselves for solutions. This book could be the
fast track.

Part I

The Outer World – Nurturing the Tangible Pillars of Wellness

Before we can explore the quiet, inner landscape of the soul, we must first build a strong and loving home for our spirit. This is the work of the Outer World. It is the tangible, practical, and deeply nourishing foundation upon which all true and lasting well-being is built.

The chapters in this first part of our journey are dedicated to nurturing the visible pillars of a healthy life. These are not rules to be followed, but invitations to engage with your world in a more conscious and loving way. Together, we will explore:

- The food we use to fuel our bodies (Nutrition)
- The joyful ways we can move (Exercise)
- The sacred art of our rest (Sleep and Dreams)
- The quality of our connections with others (Relationships)
- The tools we use to reset and rejuvenate (Retreats, Travel, and Therapies)

- The sanctuaries we create in our own homes (Creating a Healing Environment)

These are the fundamentals, the daily acts of living that we so often take for granted. By bringing our full, loving attention to these simple practices, we transform them from routine chores into sacred acts of self-respect. This is the hands-on work of wellness. It is about learning to listen to the whispers of our body so that it never has to scream.

By tending to these pillars in our outer world, we create the safety, stability, and vitality needed to embark on the deeper journey inward, which we will explore in Part II.

Let us begin.

Chapter 1

Nutrition – Fuel for Your Body and Soul

My twenty-year quest for wellness began not with gentle curiosity, but with a desperate need. For years, I felt powerless in my own body. Every month, I suffered from terrible period pains, a deep, searing agony for which I could find no solution. I remember being in my classroom, trying to teach while pacing between desks to ease the relentless cramping. I took to wearing long blazers, not as a fashion choice but as a shield, terrified that the blood and clots pouring out of me would be seen by my students if they soaked through my trousers, which, to my shame and horror, sometimes did happen.

It was out of this deep disconnect that a fierce determination was born. At forty years old, I decided that I would no longer be powerless. My journey began with studying nutrition under the guidance of the incredible Barbara Wren. It was a decision that changed my life forever. The insights I share in this chapter are the cornerstones of the philosophy that transformed my life, and I believe they can transform yours too.

The Most Important Lesson: There Is No Magic Bullet

After years of reading, studying, and experimenting, the most vital piece of wisdom I can offer you is this: you are your own best expert. Everybody is different. What works wonders for me may not work for you. Life is full of contradictions and mysteries. I know people who eat large amounts of processed food, never cook at home, and seem to be perfectly fine. We also have to take methylation into account, which is how the body uses what we put into it. It is not wise to believe everything we read about nutrition. We must let our bodies speak, and we must listen. How I feel today is directly influenced by what I ate yesterday.

I have reached the conclusion that "You can eat anything, but be prepared to live with the consequences later." The body does not lie. It speaks to us, and if we do not listen, it screams. Extremes are never healthy. I recently read about orthorexia nervosa, an excessive preoccupation with eating healthily, which I may have a mild form of. My motto is to eat in order to stay out of the hospital and nursing homes, and to be strong rather than thin. After years of striving to stay slim, I have reached a conclusion based on observation: when people are older, being too thin often leads to osteoporosis, whereas those who are a little plump seem to experience fewer problems with their bones, although they may have other challenges.

An Investment in Your Health: The Power of Quality

One of the most profound shifts in my wellness journey was realising that the quality of our food is just as important as its type. We are facing a silent crisis. The soil in which our vegetables are grown is often depleted of essential nutrients, and as a result, so are we. A fruit grower recently told me that most non-organic fruits and vegetables are injected with hormones. It is also better to eat produce that is grown close to where you live.

This is why I have become a passionate advocate for eating organic food and supporting local farmers' markets. I have been ordering from Riverford for years and am very happy with them. Organic products may be slightly more expensive, but they are an investment in your health. If you are ill, you cannot work, earn money, or truly enjoy life. As I always say, things that prolong the life of food shorten ours.

Beyond simply buying organic, it is also wise to vary what we eat so that the body benefits from diversity. Each week, I try to eat something I have not had for a while. This is much easier when we focus on seasonal produce. Visiting farmers' markets helps with this, as they sell foods you would not normally find in a supermarket, such as fresh lion's mane mushrooms or venison bones, which I use to make bone broth.

Wisdom in Practice: How to Read a Food Label

Learning how to read food labels is a non-negotiable skill. Ingredients are listed in order of quantity, so if sugar appears first, the product is mainly made of sugar. My simple rule is this: if it contains ingredients I cannot pronounce, or if it has not grown in the ground, I do not buy it. A well-known fizzy drink contains ten teaspoons of sugar, and salt is added to make you want to drink more. Low-fat foods usually contain higher amounts of sugar. Be warned, too, that sugar-free products often contain chemicals that mimic sweetness and are carcinogenic.

The Foundations of Nourishment: Your Gut, Spleen, and Soul

Illness begins in the gut, our so-called second brain. My gut has always been my weakest area. Leaky gut is increasingly common, and as we all lead hectic lives, stress has a direct and damaging effect on digestive health. Over the past two years, my main aim has been to find ways to reduce stress in my life.

Nourishing the gut is a multi-step process. Digestion begins when we think about food and when we prepare it. We must then chew our food thoroughly. This is my biggest challenge and something I have not yet managed to overcome. Chewing every mouthful 32 times feels unattainable, but I do aim to eat consciously and slowly. The better you chew, the better you digest. As I like to say, the better you chew, the better you pooh. We should chew our drinks and drink our food. The more I research, the more I encounter the idea that poor digestion reflects our inability to digest life itself. This is something I need to work on, because when we are honest, the modern world can be difficult to accept and digest, and learning how to make it more palatable is one of our greatest challenges.

Wisdom from Chinese Medicine: The Spleen and Dampness

Just as important as the gut is the spleen, which in Chinese medicine influences whether we tend towards being fat or thin. To support it, a warm, sweet drink helps it relax.

This can be made by boiling an onion, pumpkin, cabbage, and carrots for 25 minutes and drinking the resulting broth. Ancient wisdom also teaches us to avoid too many cold foods and drinks in winter, as they can create dampness in the body and weaken our digestive fire. It was a Chinese medicine doctor who, after assessing my body as a whole, confirmed that I should avoid gluten, as it caused bloating and inflammation.

The Staples: Broth and Brown Rice

Two of the most grounding and healing staples in my kitchen are bone broth and brown rice. Bone or vegetable broth nourishes both the gut and the soul. I make it, freeze it, and drink it whenever I need something or want to increase my collagen intake. The longer it simmers, the better it becomes. Once it is ready, I set the broth aside, add more vegetables to the bones, and make another batch. Organisation is key. If I have brown rice prepared, I can quickly make a soup using broth, add whatever vegetables I have on hand along with a good source of protein, and finish it with a sprinkle of coriander. The result is a balanced, nourishing meal that supports my well-being.

At the moment, when I am editing this, I am following a programme called Wildfit that looks at your relationship with food and encourages you to eat like the first humans on Earth.

Essential Support: A Guide to Intelligent and Intuitive Supplementation

While my core philosophy is to obtain nourishment from whole foods, I have come to accept that modern life requires intelligent supplementation. The silent crisis we face is that our soil is often depleted of the essential nutrients it once contained. Therefore, even if we eat a pristine diet, we are frequently still deficient in the minerals our bodies crave for optimal function. I have an entire cupboard in my kitchen dedicated to supplements, but my approach is intuitive and ever-changing, much like my diet. I believe it is beneficial to adjust what I take according to how I feel, the season we are in, or what I want to achieve.

The only supplement I take with unwavering regularity is Magnesium Breakthrough. Magnesium is perhaps the most crucial mineral, and one in which most of us are deficient. It is a true multitasker, supporting sleep, calming the mind, reducing muscle cramps, strengthening bones, lowering blood pressure, and participating in over 600 enzymatic reactions in the body. There are at least ten forms of magnesium, each with a different and vital function:

1. Magnesium Citrate: Has a laxative effect.
2. Magnesium Oxide: Supports digestion.
3. Magnesium Chloride: Can relieve heartburn and constipation.
4. Magnesium Lactate: May help with stress and anxiety.
5. Magnesium Malate: Recommended for fibromyalgia and chronic fatigue.
6. Magnesium Taurate: May help regulate blood sugar.
7. Magnesium L-Threonate: May support brain health, aiding with depression and memory loss.
8. Magnesium Sulphate, also known as Epsom salt: Used in baths for stress and sore muscles.
9. Magnesium Glycinate: Can be used to help manage anxiety, depression, and insomnia.
10. Magnesium Orotate: May support heart health.

Because of this complexity, I find a supplement such as Magnesium Breakthrough, which contains seven of these forms, to be incredibly effective and the cornerstone of my routine.

Another cornerstone of my supplement toolkit, and something I believe is essential for ageing powerfully, is a high-quality Omega-3. Its most celebrated benefit is its profound ability to combat inflammation, which is the root cause of many chronic conditions. My own journey with Omega-3 has been a powerful lesson in listening to my body. I began taking a brand called Zinzino and noticed a clear reduction in the aches and pains in my joints. To test this, I stopped taking it one summer, and the return of the aches was a clear and undeniable message from my body. This is the art of listening.

The benefits, however, extend far beyond joint health. Omega-3 fatty acids, particularly DHA, are a primary structural component of the brain and are essential for cognitive function, helping to clear brain fog, sharpen focus, and support long-term memory. They are also vital for heart health, helping to maintain healthy blood pressure and circulation. On a cellular level, they are fundamental building blocks for healthy, supple skin, promoting a natural radiance from within. They form the membranes of every cell in the body, acting as intelligent gatekeepers that allow nutrients in and usher toxins out. Because our modern diet is often high in inflammatory Omega-6 fats, supplementing with Omega-

3 is a crucial act of rebalancing. For me, it is a conscious choice to give my body the essential fats it needs to remain fluid, flexible, and resilient from the inside out.

I also apply Lugol's iodine to my skin, as many of us tend to be iodine-deficient, which is essential for supporting thyroid function. For immune support, I turn to Vitamin C when I feel I need a boost or when I remember that it helps keep me looking young, and I take L-lysine as additional support, particularly when I feel a cold sore coming on.

Part of my journey is one of constant discovery. I am currently taking slippery elm to help heal my gut lining. I also take collagen on and off, as I am still unsure whether it works for me. For moments when I crave something sweet, instead of reaching for chocolate, I sometimes take gummies such as sea moss or ashwagandha, which satisfy the craving while also providing benefits.

Finally, it is important to understand that Vitamin D is not a vitamin at all, but a hormone that the body produces itself. For this reason, I do not tend to take it regularly as a supplement. The most natural way to obtain it is through sensible sun exposure on the skin. This is also why I have reduced my use of sunglasses, as we absorb many of the sun's benefits, including the signals for Vitamin D production, through our eyes. For me, safe, non-burning sunlight exposure is the most effective supplement of all. I must also confess that in winter, when I feel I have not seen the sun for a long time, I use a Vitamin D and K2 spray under my tongue for a few days.

Another supplement I have recently been learning about and incorporating into my routine is creatine. For a long time, I associated it purely with bodybuilders, but I have come to understand it as a powerful tool for overall wellness, particularly for women as we age. Creatine is one of the most studied supplements in the world, known for its ability to improve muscle strength, power, and performance during exercise. By helping muscles produce energy more efficiently, it allows us to lift a little heavier and maintain precious muscle mass, which is crucial for long-term health, metabolism, and independence. What fascinates me most, however, are the emerging benefits beyond the gym. The brain is a high-energy organ, and creatine also acts as a fuel source for it. Research now suggests it can support cognitive function, reduce mental fatigue, and aid memory, all of which are especially important as we navigate the brain fog that can accompany menopause. It is typically taken as a simple powder mixed with water. As with any supplement, this is a personal choice, and it is always wise to consult a health professional to determine whether it is right for you. For me, it is becoming a key part of my strategy to age powerfully, both physically and mentally.

I also use certain foods as supplements. Bone broth, which I make at least once a week using either vegetables or bones, nourishes both my soul and my gut. I boil it for as long as time allows and freeze portions so I can use it when I have not been able to make a fresh batch. As I prepare it weekly, I have experimented with many methods and ingredients. What I tend to do is boil the broth for a few hours, then strain it, add more vegetables, and continue boiling the bones to create another batch. If I remember, I add apple cider vinegar, as it helps draw calcium from the bones. The best broth I make is when I am in my village in Spain, where the local butcher provides a variety of bones at very little cost. It also provides collagen that is more easily absorbed than collagen taken in powdered form.

I use herbs and spices as medicine, as this was common practice in the past. In my village, a woman lived to the age of 98 without a medical record, relying instead on herbs to heal herself. This has reinforced my belief that one of the most powerful and overlooked medicine cabinets we have is in our own kitchens, the spice rack. For thousands of years, ancient traditions such as Ayurveda and Chinese medicine have recognised that herbs and spices are not merely for flavour, but potent forms of medicine that offer gentle yet effective support for the body's natural healing processes. This wisdom is practical and accessible. For digestion, I make a simple tea by boiling fennel, cumin, coriander, and fenugreek seeds for ten minutes. It is a wonderfully soothing remedy for bloating or heartburn. I have learned that adding a small amount of cayenne pepper to food can bring remarkable benefits and may help thin the blood naturally. Spices such as turmeric are powerful anti-inflammatories, and a warm turmeric latte is one of my favourite nourishing treats after a long walk. In winter, I often turn to warming spices like ginger and cinnamon to support digestion and create a sense of inner warmth, a principle I learned from Chinese medicine. This is not about becoming an expert herbalist. It is about rediscovering the simple, profound wisdom already sitting in our cupboards. It is another layer of conscious living, a way to infuse every meal with an added measure of healing and intention.

Navigating the Modern Food World

In our modern world, we are often overfed but undernourished.

- **Protein:** As we age, we require more protein to maintain muscle, but it also helps curb cravings. I try to prevent cravings by eating whole grains such as steel-cut oats for breakfast or brown rice with pulses for lunch. Regarding meat, I choose grass-fed options and use them sparingly, more as a condiment than a main component. A portion of meat should not exceed the size of the palm of your hand. For fish, I once relied on a fishmonger who delivered fresh, wild-caught fish to my door, but this proved too expensive. Now, I select non-farmed fish at farmers' markets or supermarkets to avoid the antibiotics regularly administered to farmed fish. There was a period when avoiding meat was considered healthier, but later, nutrition experts and social media encouraged increased meat consumption. Personally, I have always enjoyed meat and was raised eating it. The most important consideration is to consume high-quality, preferably grass-fed, meat.

- **Pulses:** If you struggle to digest pulses, it may be due to improper preparation or an underperforming digestive system. Pulses should be soaked with bicarbonate of soda and a little lemon, then cooked slowly with herbs, spices, and kombu seaweed. Salt should only be added after cooking. According to Eric Edmeades from Wildfit, if you have to soak foods and spend so much time cooking them, maybe we are not supposed to consume them. Food for thought!

- **Sugar:** Of all the challenges in today's food landscape, sugar is the most insidious. I have come to view it as a substance with no nutritional value that is as addictive as cocaine. Its effects are profound and systemic. Sugar acidifies the body, creating an environment in which illness can thrive, and it is known to nourish damaged and cancerous cells. I often remind myself of a stark fact I learned during my studies: a single teaspoon of sugar can weaken the immune system for the next two hours. This knowledge transforms a simple craving into a conscious decision regarding my body's resilience. Managing sugar is a different challenge from avoiding other foods because it is pervasive and difficult to evade, particularly when out and about. I must admit that this is a habit I struggle with. Our environment often outweighs our willpower. When I am not surrounded by sugary foods, I rarely think of them, but when I encounter them, temptation can be overwhelming. I tend to crave sweets in the evening, so my simple trick is to brush my teeth immediately after an early dinner. Sometimes it works, and sometimes it does not. However, when I manage to fast or eat cleanly, the benefits are undeniable: I feel lighter, think more clearly, and experience a sense of calm. This is not about a life of deprivation; it is about conscious choice and understanding the power sugar holds over our health and habits.

- **Gluten:** The way wheat is grown in many countries renders it harmful. It has been genetically modified to be shorter, preventing breakage in the wind. My macrobiotic teacher, Diana Lopez Iriarte, says that consuming whole grains is akin to eating the potential for growth, whereas refined flour creates chaos within the body and mind. No wonder brain fog is so common. Additionally, complex carbohydrates provide essential B vitamins, which support cognitive clarity.

- **Indulgence:** As we eat cleanly, our bodies become increasingly sensitive. I follow the 80/20 rule: I eat clean 80% of the time and allow myself indulgences 20% of the time. Occasionally, enjoying foods you love prevents them from having an exaggerated impact when you do consume them.

The Body's Natural State: Removing the Cause

I have come to believe that our bodies are not designed to be sick; their natural state is one of vibrant health. Illness is rarely a mysterious affliction; it is often a logical and predictable response to overburdening. We expose our bodies to toxicity from all directions: the stress of modern life, inflammatory foods, and environmental pollutants. When the body becomes toxic, it creates an environment in which viruses and illnesses can thrive. The solution is not merely to mask symptoms with medication, which is akin to placing a piece of tape over a warning light in a car. The true remedy is to remove the cause. By providing the body with rest through fasting, a clean diet, adequate sleep, and stress reduction, we allow it to perform its natural functions: to heal, restore, and renew itself.

Deeper Nourishment: The Gut-Earth Connection

The world of probiotics is vast. I have explored prebiotics and probiotics, making my own fermented cabbage and adding miso paste to soups after boiling to preserve beneficial bacteria. I also enjoy dairy-free coconut kefir. I have noticed that I can only have very small amounts of fermented foods, as they trigger a histamine reaction in me. One of the most profound connections is Bacillus subtilis, a probiotic that reduces brain inflammation. We encounter it when we ground ourselves, touch the earth while gardening, or hug trees. This demonstrates that nourishment comes not only from what we consume but also from our relationship with the world around us.

The Sacred Art of Hydration

Drinking high-quality water is more important than consuming large quantities. Without a water filter, your body essentially becomes the filter. Maintaining an alkaline state reduces susceptibility to illness. Bancha tea in the morning helps maintain alkalinity, though I eventually changed my routine. My current method involves water with lemon, a pinch of salt, and a dash of bicarbonate of soda. Lately, to aid digestion, I prepare a tea with fennel, cumin, coriander, and fenugreek seeds, boiling them for a few minutes and sipping throughout the day.

Stress causes dehydration, and dehydration exacerbates stress. It is essential to find ways to reduce stress and maintain health. After the pandemic, many of us, myself included, realised the extreme stress in our lives and sought balance by adjusting our daily routines.

A Conscious Approach to Alcohol

Alcohol dehydrates the body and burdens the liver, but its effects extend further. It concerns me that many, particularly young people, drink to suppress emotions, and that over-consumption has become widely accepted. This is a deeply personal subject for me. I recently lost a friend due to excessive drinking, a heartbreaking reminder of the true cost of alcohol.

My practice is one of mindfulness and conscious choice. On occasion, I consume alcohol, but I select organic or high-quality wine, which tends to affect me less. The reason is clear: the liver processes both physical and emotional toxins, and excessive alcohol can negatively influence personality and provoke anger.

Since writing the previous paragraph two years ago, I have noticed that drinking alcohol causes facial redness and hot flashes, signalling that my body and liver are being overloaded with a substance that feels toxic. Having found other ways to cultivate joy, I no longer feel the need to consume alcohol. This also involves setting boundaries and learning to say no to those who enjoy drinking and may feel disappointed when I abstain.

Ultimately, this is not about prohibition, but about honesty. It is about being truthful with ourselves regarding the reasons we choose to drink and accepting the consequences of that choice on our bodies and spirits.

What Are You Really Hungry For?
The 10 Kinds of Hunger

1. Hunger for connection with yourself.
2. Nutritional hunger, the need for essential nutrients.
3. Hunger from the body, signalling the need for sleep, rest, movement, or sex.
4. Hunger for pleasure, relaxation, celebration, and enjoyment.

5. Emotional hunger, acknowledging, accepting, or expressing emotions.

6. Hunger for love, affection, acceptance, support, and understanding.

7. Hunger for safety, feeling secure regarding food, money, or basic sustenance.

8. Hunger for a sense of belonging to a cause, community, or spiritual path.

9. Hunger for intellectual growth, seeking challenges or aspirations.

10. Hunger to discover a life purpose or meaningful project.

Ultimately, our relationship with food mirrors our relationship with life. Hunger is complex. As my teacher Anna Berger explained, I often relate food to my mother's love and use it to comfort my emotions. According to my children, my mother was the best cook in the world. She would spend the entire morning preparing lunch, pouring all her love into her cooking. Her soups, broths, and stews could be smelled as soon as you entered the house. Every mouthful was a feast for the senses. She would say that cooking requires time and attention, a practice we rarely prioritise today.

I would like to believe that we are learning to love ourselves more each day and providing our bodies with what they truly need. Being conscious of the fact that how we feel today reflects how we ate yesterday, awareness and connection with our bodies are essential. My vision is that food producers will awaken to the need to create consciously produced foods and will themselves stop producing and consuming what harms us. The last decade focused on appearances; moving forward, we hope to prioritise more important aspects, such as bone density, mental wellness, and air quality. We will learn to trust our body's intelligence and thrive, rather than wasting time being unwell and suffering unnecessarily.

My Vision for the Future of Nutrition

I envision a future where we all become more conscious of what we put into our bodies. We will learn to eat with our minds, not just our palates, making choices based on how we want to feel, rather than on momentary cravings. In this future, we will eat to truly nourish ourselves, to feel energetic, vibrant, and healthy. As consumers, we hold ultimate power. By refusing processed foods, we will drive food producers to respond to our demand for real, whole foods. Proper nourishment will stabilise our blood sugar, reduce constant cravings, enhance mental clarity, and increase motivation and energy. We may even find we need less food, with one main, nourishing meal and a smaller one becoming the norm. This shift would save time and money and create a profoundly positive impact on the environment, fostering a healthier future for both ourselves and the planet.

When you feel hungry, I invite you to pause and ask yourself, "Am I truly hungry, or is this hunger for something else?" When you begin to understand what you are genuinely hungry for, you can start to give yourself what you deeply need. I believe that if you feel a real need to eat something, you should honour it. Deprivation does not serve the soul, and sometimes a little sweetness in life is necessary for joy.

Let us hope that wellness is not a fleeting trend, but a timeless investment in ourselves and a lifelong practice. The greatest harm we inflict on others often arises from neglecting our own well-being.

Your Wisdom to Go

This week's invitation: Try these three simple practices to deepen your relationship with food.

1. **Read One Label:** The next time you are at the supermarket, pick up one packaged food you

normally buy. Examine the ingredients. Do you recognise them all?

2. **Support Local:** This week, purchase one item of produce from a local shop or farmer's market. Notice the difference in quality and taste.

3. **Ask "What Am I Hungry For?":** Once this week, when you feel a craving, pause before eating and ask, "What am I truly hungry for right now?" Listen for the first answer that comes to mind.

Your Journal Prompts

An invitation for reflection: Take a few quiet moments to consider these questions.

1. When was the last time your body "whispered" to you? What was it trying to communicate?

2. What is one "inflammatory" food or habit in your life that does not serve you? What feeling or story makes it difficult to let go?

3. If you were to create a "toolkit" of three non-negotiable wellness practices, what would they be?

Chapter 2

Exercise – Moving Your Body, Changing Your Mind

We all know the feeling. It is that internal debate between the part of us that knows we should exercise and the part that would much rather stay on the sofa or in bed. For years, my full-time job and raising a family consumed all my energy, and I listened to the second voice more often than I care to admit. My relationship with exercise was inconsistent. It was not until I retired and had more time that I decided to make a genuine investment in myself and became more focused. What I have learned is that exercise is not a punishment for what you ate or a chore to be endured. It is a celebration of what your body can do, and one of the most powerful tools we have for instantly changing our state of mind. When we exercise, we release endorphins, which make us feel good.

It is important to distinguish between general activity and dedicated exercise. Activity differs from exercise; walking or doing household chores are not formal exercise, but they are still beneficial for our health. The secret is not to force yourself into a gruelling routine you hate. Rather, the key is to find joy in movement. When you shift your perspective from "I have to do this" to "I get to do this," everything changes. This chapter explores the many ways we can move our bodies, not only to build physical strength but also to cultivate a deep and lasting sense of well-being.

Finding Your Joyful Movement

For years, I believed exercise had to be a serious, structured affair at the gym. I was wrong. The most sustainable form is the one that brings a smile to your face. For me, that discovery was a lifeline. After my mother's death, my body felt heavy with grief that was almost physical. The pain was literally in my heart, a constant, dense ache accompanied by the profound feeling of being an orphan in the world.

It was in a Monday Zumba class that I first felt a glimmer of light. The teacher, Maria, wears colourful leotards and tells us that anything goes; we are just there to party. I love it because we all leave with big smiles on our faces. In the class, there are young, old, thin, and overweight women, and we all do our own thing. I sometimes think that if we filmed the class, it would resemble a comedy. In that hour of joyful, uninhibited movement, something began to shift. The music and laughter allowed me to physically move the grief that had been lodged in my heart. I left feeling lighter than I had in months.

Joyful movement can be found anywhere. Lately, I am obsessed with the song "Flowers" by Miley Cyrus. I love to play and dance while doing housework. My husband taught me to enjoy music, and now I play it in the background to raise my vibration. We even have a karaoke machine, and although I cannot sing, I try "My Heart Will Go On" by Céline Dion. I feel amazing afterwards, as it encourages deep, intentional breathing.

Joyful movement can also build community. When three of my neighbours mentioned they felt lonely, we organised a tea party for our street. The result? My lovely 82-year-old neighbour, Amarik, invited me to join her Kundalini yoga sessions every Wednesday. Now, a small group of us gathers regularly. We pay £5, which we donate to charity, and after the lesson, we share tea, Indian snacks, and conversation. This shared movement has woven us into a community that sustains us. This group also introduced me to a charity run through the Lyons organisation to raise funds for good causes. I am normally reluctant to donate, as I feel contributions seldom reach those who need them, but here I feel confident it does. The last event I attended raised money to help Indian girls learn a trade, empowering them to earn a living. I thought that was excellent because if you give someone a fish, they eat for a day, but if you teach them to fish, they can eat for a lifetime.

The Sacred Art of Walking

One of the most effective and accessible forms of exercise is walking in nature. In Japan, the practice of Shinrin-yoku, or "forest bathing," is so revered that doctors prescribe it. They understand that trees release substances that improve health, reduce stress, strengthen the heart, and clear the mind. Walking burns body fat, strengthens muscles, increases energy, and improves posture and flexibility.

I also love walking with friends. A "walk and talk" on Hampstead Heath is one of my absolute favourite activities, combining deep conversation and what I call "free therapy" with gentle movement. We are fortunate to have so many beautiful green spaces in London. Our walks always end at a lovely spot for lunch or a warm turmeric latte, a perfect, nourishing conclusion to a perfect outing.

Building a Strong Foundation

While joyful movement is essential for the spirit, building a strong physical foundation is crucial for long-term health. I view my gym membership not as a cost but as an investment in my well-being. When I leave, I feel a sense of wellness, and that is what I am paying for. On Mondays and Thursdays, I do 20 minutes of a routine called 10X, which involves six machines, twelve repetitions each, done three times, increasing the weight as I grow stronger.

My latest discovery at the gym has been a profound and joyful practice called dance meditation. We gather in a darkened room, each with our own set of headphones, creating an intimate personal experience within a collective space. The music begins, and for an hour, we are guided to move, jump, sway, and dance with complete freedom. The purpose is not to perform but to physically shake off stagnant emotions, stress, and the stories that become lodged in our bodies. We emerge from the darkness feeling lighter, clearer, and profoundly liberated, as if a heavy weight has been lifted off the dance floor. The magic does not end there. This invigorating release is followed by a deeply restorative sound bath. We lie down, wrapped in blankets, and allow the vibrational frequencies of crystal bowls, gongs, and chimes to wash over us. It is a form of cellular massage, a vibrational healing that calms the nervous system and integrates the emotional release from the dance. This combination is a powerful reminder that healing can be both active and receptive, joyful and peaceful, and that sometimes the best way to find our centre is to first allow ourselves to completely let go.

Afterwards, I visit the spa for hot and cold therapy. I have learned to be kind and gentle with myself, staying in the freezing plunge pool for only a minute. It is a small but profound shift from forcing my body to honouring it. When I emerge from the spa and no longer feel the cold in winter, I tell myself I am investing in wellness.

Having a strong core is also non-negotiable. My wonderful teacher, Talia, says, "If you do not want back problems later on, you must strengthen the core." Her class is incredibly challenging, but in that challenge, I am building resilience. I am careful not to push myself too hard and risk injury, yet I push enough to grow stronger. This is not about achieving a particular appearance; it is about creating a strong, healthy body that will serve as my vehicle through life, ensuring mobility, independence, and supporting digestion as I age.

One of the most profound and unexpected lessons I have learned on my wellness journey came from the naturopath

Barbara O'Neill. She explained that persistent digestive issues, such as bloating, acid reflux, or the sensation that food simply sits in our stomachs, often stem from weak stomach muscles rather than the food itself. This resonated with me deeply. The stomach is essentially a muscular bag designed to churn, squeeze, and mix food with powerful digestive acids. If the surrounding core and stomach muscles are weak, often due to a sedentary lifestyle, the stomach cannot perform this essential churning effectively. As a result, food may sit for too long, leading to fermentation, gas, and discomfort. This simple truth reframes the problem; the solution is not solely about what we eat but also about building physical strength from the outside in. It is a powerful reminder that the strength of our core is directly linked to the digestive strength of our gut.

The Wisdom of Stillness: The Power of Yin Yoga

While some forms of exercise focus on generating heat and moving quickly, I have discovered that some of the most profound work occurs in stillness. This, for me, is the true power of Yin yoga, a slow, meditative practice taught by my wonderful daughter-in-law, Rebecca. Rather than flowing from one pose to the next, you hold positions for several minutes at a time, targeting not only the muscles but also the deeper connective tissues and fascia, where our bodies are believed to store tension, trauma, and years of unprocessed emotions. This practice has been transformative for me. After decades of my body operating in a "fight or flight" mode, Yin yoga demands surrender. You cannot rush. You have no choice but to slow down, connect deeply with your body, and simply be present with whatever feelings arise. The result is a profound physical and emotional release. Afterwards, you feel deeply relaxed, and your sleep improves. I truly believe this form of yoga represents the future of the practice—not as a replacement for other forms, but as an essential antidote to our fast-paced world. It is the practice of slowing down, listening to the subtle whispers of our body, and finally releasing what we have been holding for so long.

Wisdom in Practice: A Note on Cardio and Cortisol

I approach excessive cardiovascular exercise with caution. While cardio is excellent for heart health, too much can elevate cortisol levels—a stress hormone. For women, especially during midlife, managing cortisol is essential. Chronically high cortisol can contribute to stubborn belly fat, anxiety, and sleep disruption. Balance is key. A brisk walk, a joyful dance class, or short bursts of higher-intensity exercise are all excellent. To help balance cholesterol, elevating the feet is said to be beneficial, so I do this when I remember or while in the sauna. I always say that the most important aspect of exercise is to avoid injury, because if you are sidelined, you may not be able to exercise for months, which can set you back significantly.

Beyond the Gym: Sun, Brain, and a Life in Motion

Wellness is holistic, and some of the most powerful practices occur outside of structured classes. I view sunbathing as a form of exercise. As a Spaniard living in London, I sometimes feel like a tropical flower in the North Pole! When the sun appears, I make a beeline for it, recharging like a battery. Since the widespread use of sunscreen, cases of skin cancer have paradoxically increased. Vitamin D is not a vitamin; it is a hormone that the body produces. An American scientist once remarked that, rather than spending money on vitamin D supplements, one could use that money to travel somewhere sunny in midwinter. I know this is easier said than done, but travelling during the low season may also be more cost-effective.

Perhaps the most vital form of exercise is simply remaining in motion. Sitting has been described as the new smoking, and I find this to be profoundly true. Our bodies were not designed to be sedentary. My personal philosophy has become wonderfully simple: I either walk or lie down. It is in the stagnant, seated world that our vitality begins to diminish.

Wellness extends beyond the physical. Just as we train our muscles, we must exercise our brains. I have always disliked puzzles and Sudoku, finding them frustrating. Instead, I have discovered a more creative and powerful mental exercise: the practice of manifestation. This involves using my imagination and intellect to consciously shape my life. It requires practice, but the main steps are as follows: first, be clear about what you want; if uncertain, be general and let the universe handle the details. Second, pay attention to your words, as they act as commands sent into the universe. Third, and most importantly, infuse your thoughts with emotion and feel the desired outcome as if it is happening now. Finally, follow the signs and synchronicities that appear. This practice has revealed a profound truth to me: a goal is a place we come from, not a destination. I remind myself: I am healthy; my digestion is excellent. I visualise my life as if I have already achieved my goals. This is not mere wishful thinking; it is a daily mental exercise that aligns my energy and actions with the reality I wish to create.

I have noticed that bars and pubs are closing, while gyms, spas, yoga studios, and wellness centres offering IV drips are opening. Young people are increasingly choosing to invest in their health and well-being, which is incredibly encouraging.

A Vision for the Future of Exercise

I envision a future in which our relationship with exercise is completely transformed. Exercise will no longer be a chore but an integrated and joyful part of daily life, something we do naturally, like brushing our teeth. In this future, our approach will be intelligent and intentional. We will move beyond generic routines to embrace personalised programmes that target precisely what we aim to achieve, whether building strength, increasing flexibility, or enhancing cognitive function. We will learn to optimise our fitness by discovering the precise movements and methods that yield maximum results with minimal effort. Imagine having a personalised programme that intelligently adapts to our age and life stage, ensuring our bodies can thrive, not merely survive, in every season of life. This is the future of movement: it will not be about punishment or pain but about smart, sustainable, and joyful practices that allow us to inhabit our bodies with power and grace. I might even venture to say that through mindful exercise, we can defy ageing.

A Final Thought

For those who dislike exercise, my most compassionate advice is simple: start small. The most important thing is to move. Walk. Do something manageable that fits your daily routine. Do not worry about the outcome; simply notice how you feel afterwards. Exercise releases endorphins, a powerful feel-good factor. Let that feeling guide you. Movement is a conversation with your body, not a command. I invite you to explore, to play, and to discover the unique ways your body loves to move.

Your Wisdom to Go

This week's invitation: Movement is a gift, not a chore. Try these three simple practices to bring more joyful exercise into your life.

1. **Try a Movement Snack**: You do not need an hour. When your favourite song plays, get up and dance for

three full minutes. That is your "movement snack." Notice how it shifts your energy.

2. **Schedule a "Walk and Talk"**: Instead of meeting a friend for coffee, invite them on a walk. Combining connection with movement is one of the most effective ways to boost well-being.

3. **Do a "Fight or Flight" Check-In**: Twice today, pause what you are doing. Is your jaw clenched? Are your shoulders raised towards your ears? Are you breathing shallowly? If so, take three slow, deep breaths and consciously tell your body it is safe to relax.

Your Journal Prompts

An invitation for reflection: Take a few quiet moments to ponder these questions.

1. What is your oldest belief about exercise? Where did it originate? Does it still serve you?

2. Describe an activity that makes you feel genuinely joyful and graceful in your body. How could you incorporate just ten minutes of that feeling into your life this week?

3. In what area of your life are you currently "pushing" when your body might be asking for more "gentleness"? What would being kinder to yourself in that area look like?

Chapter 3

Sleep and Dreams – The Art of Restoration

A friend of ours, a millionaire, once came to stay with us. One evening, he shared something that has stayed with me ever since. He told me, "Lucia, no matter how much money you have in the bank, the most important things in life are a good night's sleep, going to the toilet properly, and not being in pain." I have never forgotten that. Sleep is a form of wealth that cannot be bought, a precious commodity that is absolutely essential to our well-being.

Yet, I know that for many of us, it feels like an elusive treasure. For years, I survived on five or six hours of sleep a night, and I always felt like I was running on empty. When you do not sleep properly, you cannot function, and you tend to take things out of proportion. Lack of sleep can also make you overeat, as it affects the hormones ghrelin and leptin, which control appetite. In my conversations with so many others, I hear the same quiet desperation of a world that is sleep-deprived.

Through my own journey, I have come to believe that sleep is a mystery. There is no single, infallible solution. The key is not to conquer sleep, but to create a loving invitation for it to arrive. I have learned that it is not just about the quantity of hours we get, but the quality of our rest and the feeling of being truly restored when we wake.

Creating a Sanctuary for Sleep

Our bodies are creatures of habit, and they respond to the environment we create. If we want to invite deep rest, we must first build a sanctuary that feels safe and conducive to it.

Light, or the lack of it, is one of the most powerful signals we can send to our bodies. It is crucial to make your bedroom as dark as possible to encourage melatonin production. I even have a switch that turns off all the appliances in my bedroom at a certain time in the evening to eliminate any subtle light. Equally important is exposing yourself to the sun or bright light first thing in the morning. This simple act helps to set your internal clock.

My winding-down ritual is a key part of this. I dim the lights and sometimes drink a warm, caffeine-free herbal tea. I would never take sleeping pills; in fact, doctors do not prescribe them as often anymore, and I am pleased about that. A small comfort I have found is using a magnesium spray on the soles of my feet. I massage it in, feeling the tension release from my body. I also use eucalyptus oil sometimes, but not all the time, because the body gets used to it and the remedy becomes less effective.

What we consume also plays a significant role. Our liver affects our sleep, so relaxing foods such as wholegrain cereals can help. Conversely, salty or sugar-laden foods cause our liver to contract and can disrupt our sleep.

The Mind-Sleep Connection

I suppose that when we cannot sleep, we need to look for the cause. Some causes occur at night, such as sleep apnoea, snoring, or restless leg syndrome. People who suffer from these conditions feel sleepy during the day because they do not experience the deep sleep that repairs the body and mind. We also have secondary causes, such as having a baby or being in menopause, which is where I am at.

But for most of us, the true battlefield for sleep is often in our own minds. When your day is stressful, it is incredibly challenging to switch off. This brings me to the great paradox of sleep: the more you try to get it, the less you achieve it. When you are awake in the middle of the night, time seems to slow down. The thought that often hooks me is, "It is only three o'clock! I will be so exhausted tomorrow." Of course, that thought is the very thing that fuels the anxiety and keeps me awake. One of the perks of being retired is that I do not have to set an alarm clock in the morning, so I can go back to sleep if I wake early, although sometimes I cannot.

In those moments, I sometimes try a trick I learned from one of my students on a school trip. I saw her shaking her head from side to side on the plane, sitting next to me, and within minutes, she fell asleep. She told me that is what she did when she wanted to sleep. Now, when my mind is racing, I sometimes lie there and gently shake my head. It is a physical interruption to a mental loop. When something is truly worrying you, however, all the theories and tactics go out of the window. In those moments, the only real remedy is self-compassion and taking it easy the following day.

The Hidden World of Dreams: Restoration and Travel

When we sleep, we do more than just rest. We restore our bodies and our minds, and we travel to another world. This is the hidden, magical dimension of sleep: the world of dreams.

Dreaming is an essential part of our nightly restoration, helping to cleanse our subconscious mind. For a while, I kept a dream journal by my bed. The secret to remembering a dream is to capture it before you move. Dreams are like an emotional thermometer; they reveal how we are truly feeling and can offer insights or solutions. We need to pay attention to recurring dreams, especially those of travel, houses, or moving, as they could indicate changes in our lives.

A Vision for the Future of Sleep

My dream for the future of sleep is that we will all learn to harness its true power. I envision a time when we can reach such a deep level of communication with our subconscious mind that we can simply instruct it to give us a perfect night's rest. Imagine, as you lie your head on the pillow, giving your subconscious its nightly assignments: to address any problems or worries in your life, to dream and resolve emotional issues, and then to wake you at a specified time with a solution. In this future, we would all wake up feeling completely refreshed and rested, ready to be our best selves. Before even getting out of bed, we could use that clear, creative state to visualise our day ahead, setting the stage for synchronicities to happen, allowing us to move through our hours with productivity, creativity, and a profound sense of calm. This is the ultimate potential of sleep: not just as rest for the body, but as a nightly reset for the soul.

A Final Thought

The way we end the day before going to sleep supports our sleep. And the way we start our day after waking dictates how our day will unfold. This creates a beautiful, continuous cycle of intention, where our nights and days nourish each other.

Ultimately, sleep rejuvenates us. I was once told a story about a French Queen. Before a big party, she would sleep for two full days. When she emerged, she looked impossibly amazing and youthful. For me, this story is the ultimate testament to the power of rest. When I sleep well, I not only feel better but look younger; my face appears more refreshed, and my spirit feels lighter. It is the greatest gift we can give ourselves and something we need to consciously cultivate in our lives.

I have a few remedies for when I am travelling or when the full moon seems to affect my sleep, such as taking a botanical oil or Rescue Remedy.

Be gentle with yourself on this journey. Your body knows how to sleep. Our work is simply to create the safe and loving conditions for it to do so. If we learn to live softly, our lives will be less stressful, and sleep will come more easily.

Where do we go when we sleep? Is life just a dream?

Your Wisdom to Go

This week's invitation: Try these three simple practices to begin building a more loving relationship with sleep.

1. **Meet the Morning Sun:** For the next three days, as soon as you wake up, spend two minutes by a window and let the morning light hit your face. Notice how it makes you feel.

2. **Create a Gratitude Sandwich:** Tonight, before sleeping, write or mentally list three things you were grateful for today. Do the same when you wake, before getting out of bed.

3. **Keep a Dream Catcher:** Place a notebook and pen by your bed. If you wake with a dream fresh in your mind, write down any images, feelings, or words you remember before doing anything else. Do not analyse it; just capture it.

Your Journal Prompts

An invitation for reflection: Take a few quiet moments to ponder these questions.

1. What is your oldest or most stubborn belief about sleep? (e.g., "I am just a bad sleeper.") Where did this belief come from?

2. Think of your bedroom. What is one small change you could make this week to make it feel more like a sanctuary for rest?

3. If you were not allowed to worry about tomorrow between the hours of 10 p.m. and 6 a.m., what would you do with that mental space instead?

Chapter 4

Relationships – The Quality of Your Connections

If there is one lesson my over sixty years on this earth have taught me, it is this: the quality of your life depends greatly on the quality of your relationships. That is why this chapter is so vitally important. I have come to believe that our relationships exist to make us conscious, not necessarily happy. Our connections with others are not merely a part of our lives; they are the very fabric of them. They are here to teach us, to challenge us, and ultimately, to help us grow. Every person who enters our lives serves as a mirror and a teacher, offering lessons that we all must learn. As we grow older, drama becomes increasingly unacceptable as it drains too much energy.

Happier people usually practise gratitude, are attuned to their feelings, cultivate strong relationships, and forgive themselves and others, recognising that people will let us down, just as we will let others down. They pursue personal growth, and we often become like the five people we spend the most time with, which we need to be mindful of.

When my daughter was heartbroken, I felt her pain as if it were my own, reminding me that we are only as happy as our least happy child. Through that experience, I consolidated a crucial lesson in boundaries: it is not necessary to take on the suffering of others. We all have our own paths to follow. This is the delicate dance of all relationships: learning where we end and another person begins. When we suffer for others, we do not ease their pain; instead, we lower our own vibration, which we need to maintain at a high level so we can lift them rather than descend to their level.

The Master Teacher: Your Partner

"If I accept the fact that my relationships are here to make me conscious, rather than happy, then my relationships become a wonderful self-mastery tool that keeps realigning me with my higher purpose for living." — Eckhart Tolle.

Your romantic partner will be your greatest teacher. This is a profound truth, but it runs contrary to the fantasy we are sold from childhood. The old fairy tales have done us a great disservice. Marriage in those stories was a destination, a "happily ever after." In the past, for many, it was a practical arrangement that guaranteed a roof over their head and food on the table. Today, thankfully, we have more choices, but that freedom brings its own challenges. What is undeniable is that one of the most important decisions you will make is who you marry.

Relationships, like sleep, remain a great mystery. I have seen many couples who seemed happy but divorced, and I have friends who constantly argue yet remain together for decades. I have concluded that if you have a soul contract with someone, you will stay together through thick and thin because your souls have chosen to learn certain lessons. The suffering experienced in relationships is not a sign of failure; it is a sign that you are learning. Your partner will, with perfect and often painful precision, mirror back to you all your unhealed wounds.

This often occurs because we subconsciously choose our partners based on familiar patterns. We tend to marry our father or our mother. I believe I married my mother in some ways, as she was a Scorpio like my husband, and they share many of the same traits. We attract what we know.

Sadly, it is often in divorce that you truly come to know your partner, when love can turn into hatred. It is a stark reminder of the fine line between our most intense emotions. A good marriage, I believe, is simply one in which you do not give up. The commitment to navigating the messy, challenging, and beautiful struggles together is what forges a bond that lasts. As I get older, I increasingly appreciate having someone with whom I can simply exist, a companion and presence. Perhaps because I have never lived alone, I feel I would find it challenging.

I have come to understand that arguing is futile, as we will not change another person's mind. We argue because we are desperately trying to prove that we are right about a belief we hold. The fundamental problem is that the other person is doing exactly the same. We are left in a stalemate, having wasted precious energy with no hope of a different outcome. A more powerful approach is to seek understanding rather than victory. Instead of fighting back, we can practise the art of listening and simply say, "I hear you." It is not an admission of defeat, but an act of grace that validates the other person's reality without compromising our own. I have learned that I will always prioritise peace of mind over being right. It is also wise never to argue when angry. It is far better to take a walk, reflect until you calm down, and ask yourself, "What needs are not being met?"

before returning to the conversation. This conscious choice to step away from conflict is the true path to connection.

The Chosen Family: The Power of Friendship and Community

While we cannot choose our family, we can choose our friends. My mother used to say, "You can never have enough friends," and at 97, she was indeed a wise lady. Nurturing healthy friendships brings a sense of joy and connection that is essential to our well-being. It is helpful to remember that friendships can take different forms. You can have friends for a reason, such as attending the same gym; for a season, like completing a course; or for life, those who have been there from the start and continue to support you. I recently heard Mel Robbins say that every seven years, you will have a new set of friends, which reminded me not to become overly attached and to remember that life is like a train. A few people travel with us for the entire journey, while others join us for only a few stops.

When you live abroad and away from your family, your friends become your family. After living in London for more than forty years, I have had the privilege of weaving a rich and varied tapestry of community that sustains me. It is a testament to the power of shared experiences over time. I still meet with friends from my children's playgroup to celebrate birthdays, a bond forged in those early days of motherhood. I have friends from my children's primary and secondary schools, women who navigated the same parenting milestones alongside me. My neighbours have become an essential support system, helping with the practicalities of daily life. My nutrition friends, my "Nymphs of North London," are my go-to for advice and inspiration. I am still connected to many colleagues from 25 years of teaching. I am part of La Peña, a group of Spanish-speaking residents in London that keeps me connected to my roots. More recently, I found my tribe in Rowsanara and Christine, whom I met at a writer's workshop. For the past four years, we have walked together in the world of writing, supporting each other's creative journeys. Each of these groups forms a thread, and together they create a strong, beautiful fabric of connection that has become my chosen family.

A true friendship is a sacred space. It is vital to have friends who inspire you and whom you inspire in return. I find it enriching to have friends of different age groups; my older friends impart wisdom, while the younger ones provide energy. I have a theory that we enjoy watching soap operas because, in the past, our neighbours provided entertainment. Today, we often do not even know our neighbours, so soap operas fill that gap. It reflects our deep need for social connection and storytelling, a need that men, I have observed, generally find harder to fulfil, as they often struggle to maintain and cultivate friendships.

Pets, too, can become our chosen family. I was never an animal lover until an old man at my allotment placed a tiny kitten in my hand and said, "Take her home, or the foxes will eat her." And just like that, Mishi entered my life. She has taught me so much about unconditional love. When I come home and do not see her for a while, I begin to worry, and my heart almost stops. Many of my friends have dogs, and I recognise their loyalty, though I feel it is akin to having half a baby. I also feel that we are humanising pets, and we must remain aware of this.

The Unbreakable Bonds: Family and Chosen Kin

While friends can become our chosen family, there is a unique and unbreakable bond we share with our relatives. I always say that friends come and go, but our relatives will always be our blood. They are the keepers of our history, the people who know our stories from the very beginning.

I have come to believe that being a parent is the most important job we will ever undertake, yet it is the one for which nobody truly prepares us. We are not just raising children; we are shaping the citizens of the future, and they are our greatest legacy. I feel this deeply, and I poured my heart and soul into the task. I became a "tiger mum," particularly with my daughter, encouraging her in music, tutoring, and additional classes because, at the time, I believed I was doing what was best for her. I am incredibly proud of my children, who have grown into decent, productive human beings, but my perspective has softened with time. I have learned that our ultimate role is not to control them, but to prepare them for life. We must teach them to care for themselves so that they are not a burden to their family or society. Yet the most important lessons are not taught through words. Our children emulate what they see us do, not what we tell them to do. In the end, we must accept that they are not ours to keep. Children are like boats lent to us for a few years, and our sacred duty is to prepare them to be seaworthy, so that we may one day return them to the sea. They have their own journey to complete. I believe that our children choose us to teach us the lessons we most need to learn, and that is a humbling and beautiful thought.

My relationship with my sisters-in-law is a testament to the work I have done in cultivating conscious relationships. A relationship with a sister-in-law can be a tricky one, but I have always made a point of maintaining harmony. Our connection is built on a foundation of deep respect, and having faced many of life's challenges together has forged a quiet understanding between us. It reassures us that we will always be there for each other, and that feeling is profoundly comforting.

My cousin, Asun, is very close to my heart. She is not just family; she is my best friend. Our mothers were sisters, and our fathers were brothers, and we grew up so close that our bond transcends both distance and time. We know with unshakeable certainty that we will support each other through thick and thin. She has endured much, yet she has grown into a wise, kind, and generous person who keeps our family together. She is our superglue.

Then there is my niece, Rakel, and her two beautiful daughters. They are more than just my niece and great-nieces; they are the precious link to my brother, who passed away. In them, I see his legacy, and our connection is a sacred thread that preserves his memory in my heart. These relationships have taught me a profound truth: our relatives are the souls chosen to walk alongside us, to guide us, and to teach us the deepest lessons of love and loyalty in ways we could never have imagined.

The Most Important Relationship: The One with Yourself

For years, I experienced difficulties in my relationships because I did not know how to set boundaries. Once I understood that boundaries are not about controlling others but about managing my own behaviour, my life became infinitely more peaceful. All external relationships reflect the one we have with ourselves. Intimacy means, into me I see.

This inner relationship extends beyond people. It includes our relationship with concepts and authority. When I was a child, I was threatened with the 'police coming.' I developed a fear of the police and figures of authority, which has influenced my perception of all the bosses I have had, and has probably not served me well. It is not that my parents were cruel; many people feared the police after the Spanish Civil War, and that fear was passed down through generations. It is a powerful example of an inherited story that I have had to confront within myself.

We all feel lonely at times, especially after COVID, when we began to enjoy our own company and became more insular. I believe we all carry an emptiness inside that is difficult to fill. We are torn between the enjoyment of community and friendship and the desire to avoid taking on other people's issues when we already have enough of our own. I will always remember how my dearest friend Sally sent me a link to her amazing yoga class, which helped me connect with her, my body and other members of the class.

For me, a significant challenge has been the Fear of Missing Out (FOMO). It is the anxiety we feel when we think we should be elsewhere, doing something more exciting. I am learning to notice it and to gently remind myself that we are always where we are meant to be. I am learning to embrace JOMO, which is the Joy of Missing Out.

Ultimately, we must become our own best friend. We are the person we will spend the most time with, after all. The greatest work we will ever undertake is learning to be kinder to ourselves and to heal the generational wounds we carry.

A Vision for the Future of Relationships

In an ideal world, the future of relationships will be one in which we instinctively feel that we are in this together, that we are all one. We will live by the profound truth that if you do well, I do well too. In this future, we will attract those who resonate at the same frequency as us, and our connections will be based on mutual respect and universal love. We will learn to trust our instincts more, allowing them to guide us toward people who will enrich and inspire our lives. We will not rush into marriage but will instead wait with patience and wisdom until we find our soul mate, the person with whom we can truly grow together. In this paradigm, there will be no need for divorce, which in turn will give our children the most precious gift of all: a secure and safe environment in which to thrive. This is not merely a dream; it is a possibility we can begin to create, one conscious connection at a time.

A Final Thought

Every relationship is a sacred assignment. Your partner, your children, your relatives, your friends, even your pets; they are all here to help you see yourself more clearly. When you begin to view every connection as a gift, every challenge as a lesson, and every person as a teacher, your entire world transforms. The love you seek from others can only be found by first discovering it within yourself.

Your Wisdom to Go

This week's invitation: Try these three simple practices to bring more awareness and intention to your relationships.

1. **Practice Active Appreciation:** Choose one person in your life. For the next two days, make a conscious effort to notice something you genuinely appreciate about them and tell them what it is.

2. **Check Your Own Energetic Pulse:** The next time you finish a conversation, pause for a moment. Ask yourself: "How do I feel right now? Energised, drained, or neutral?"

3. **Schedule a Date with Yourself:** Set aside 30 minutes this week for a "date" with yourself, a solo walk, a cup of tea without your phone, or listening to your favourite music.

Your Journal Prompts

An invitation for reflection: Take a few quiet moments to consider these questions.

1. Think of a person in your life who challenges you. Ask yourself: "What might this person be here to teach me?"

2. Who in your life makes you feel most seen and appreciated? What is one thing you can do this week to reflect that same energy back to them?

3. If your relationship with yourself were a friendship, how would you describe it? What is one thing you could do today to be a better friend to yourself?

Chapter 5

Retreats, Travel, and Therapies – Tools for a Reset

There is a fundamental difference between a holiday and a retreat. Most of us go on holiday seeking an escape, and we return feeling tired, overfed, and overstimulated, as if we need another holiday just to recover. A retreat, however, is not an escape; it is a return. It is an intentional act of stepping away from the noise of our lives in order to reconnect with ourselves. You come back feeling refreshed, rejuvenated, and ready to engage with your life from a place of renewed clarity. This chapter is dedicated to the external tools—the places, journeys, and healing modalities—that have helped me reset my health and reconnect with my spirit.

The Power of the Reset: My Journey with Retreats

My journey as a nutritionist began with a single lecture at Regents College, where Amanda Hamilton spoke about detox retreats. In the afternoon, a speaker named Barbara Wren took the stage, and as she spoke, something deep inside me clicked into place. I was so inspired that I decided to study nutrition with her, a decision that would change the course of my life forever.

This experience contrasts sharply with my 40th birthday trip. For that milestone, I went to St Lucia in the Caribbean. I ate too much and drank too many cocktails, but a chance encounter with an American actress convinced me to buy a bikini. She told me I had a good figure but needed to lose 10 kilograms, which set me on the path to look after my body. She will never know the effect her comment had on me.

Twenty years later, my desire for my 60th birthday was not indulgence, but healing. We chose Kamalaya in Thailand. It was magical. The scenery, with its infinity pools that seemed to merge with the sea, was like paradise. We were not allowed to use our phones, and although this was difficult at first, it soon became the greatest gift. A deep inner peace began to settle in. Each therapist helped me uncover more about myself. One yoga teacher told me that if I wanted a flat stomach, I had to keep pushing it in. During a Pranayama session, a therapist explained that the mind controls the body, but the breath controls the mind. She taught me to breathe using the stomach, chest, and throat. The Qi Gong master said the place had a soul, and one of my most cherished memories was attending a tea ceremony with Master San Bao, who taught us how to truly appreciate a cup of tea.

Slowing down, being in touch with your body and your emotions, and removing yourself from external noise can bring immense well-being into our lives.

A Deeper Journey: Lessons from Travel

Sometimes, a journey is not a retreat but a profound cultural immersion that teaches you in a different way. Such was my trip to Japan for our 40th wedding anniversary in 2025. The experience was a lesson in grace and intention. The food is treated like a work of art, and this care extends to the people. I was humbled by their helpfulness; when I needed to buy nappies for my granddaughter, a shop assistant personally walked me to the pharmacy next door while another waited for me with my shopping trolley. It is a culture built on consideration for others. The silence in public places is calming. Of course, it is not a perfect country, but when I returned, I wanted to bring some of the energy I felt there, the quiet respect, the mindful care, and the sense of community, into my own life. This is the true gift of travel.

Sometimes, you do not have to travel far to enjoy such experiences. Since obtaining my sixty-plus Freedom Pass, I have fallen in love with London. I explore different areas with my friends, and we delight in walking around and discovering new places. Yesterday, I had a magical day with my lovely friend Simy, visiting an astrology shop, having lunch in Mayfair, and enjoying tea at Sketch. Every area transports me to a different feeling.

Having had a holiday home near Alicante for over twenty years, which I recently sold, I have learned two lessons. First, we come with nothing, and we leave with nothing, so we should enjoy things without attachment. Second, when you have a place in another country, you feel as though you live two lives. Travel also reminds us to stay mobile. I remember an old man on a tour in Morocco who refused to leave the coach as he could not walk. That day, I told myself that I must get out there while I can.

The Inner Journey: Lessons from the Camino de Santiago

Sometimes, a journey is more than a trip; it is a pilgrimage that mirrors the path of life itself. Last year, I walked the final 140 kilometres of the Camino de Santiago, the ancient pilgrim route through Spain. It was a profound experience, filled with moments of both intense challenge and incredible beauty. As I walked, I realised that the Camino is the perfect metaphor for life: there are uphill struggles that test your endurance, long, flat stretches that can feel monotonous, and breathtaking vistas that fill your soul with awe. There were moments when I wanted to give up, but I persevered, and the feeling of reaching the cathedral in Santiago de Compostela was an overwhelming wave of accomplishment, gratitude, and release.

Along the way, I fell completely in love with Galicia, its mystical green landscapes, the warmth of its people, and the simple perfection of its food. They say that the Camino is addictive and, once it gets into your blood, it calls you back. I understand this now. It is not just a walk; it is a spiritual reset, a journey that strips you down to your essence and reminds you of your own strength and resilience. I may well undertake another path in the future, to once again walk my way back to myself.

A Toolkit for the Soul: Therapies that Have Healed Me

I believe that Western medicine is invaluable for accidents and emergencies. However, it has increasingly become more about sick care than health care. It typically provides medication that addresses symptoms rather than the underlying cause. This realisation led me to explore other paths to well-being.

I have tried a wide variety of therapies in my quest to feel my best. None has been a total miracle, but most have been helpful in one way or another. Each has become a valuable tool.

One of the most extravagant yet worthwhile investments I have ever made in my well-being sits in the small office we built at the back of our garden. Several years ago, I treated myself to a personal infrared sauna, which has become my sacred Sunday ritual. Unlike a traditional sauna that heats the air around you, an infrared sauna uses a special type of light to warm your body directly from the inside out. The experience is a gentle, penetrating heat that feels profoundly healing. This deep warmth helps to release toxins through sweat, soothes sore muscles, and, most importantly for me, calms the nervous system. Stepping out of that gentle heat after a session, feeling cleansed, renewed, and completely relaxed, is the perfect end to my week. My personal hope is that it will also help with the stubborn visceral fat that can accumulate around our organs as we age. For me, it is more than just a piece of equipment; it is a small, personal sanctuary where I can close the door on the world and allow my body to rest, repair, and rejuvenate on a cellular level.

- **Homoeopathy:** In my journey through different healing modalities, I have found a consistent and gentle ally in homoeopathy. It is a system of medicine based on the principle of "like cures like," using highly diluted natural substances to stimulate the body's own healing mechanisms. I have turned to it on many occasions, and it has often helped when nothing else would. After my mum passed away, the grief manifested as a return of my old digestive issues. I started using homoeopathy again, and it truly helped to calm and rebalance my system. The key, I have learned, is to find a skilled, intuitive practitioner who can guide you to the right remedies for your specific constitution and symptoms. For me, homoeopathy is a beautiful reminder that healing does not always have to be aggressive; sometimes, the most profound shifts come from the subtlest of nudges.

- **Self-hypnotherapy**: This is one of the most powerful tools I have used in my quest to heal my inner world. It is a practice I have employed to consciously decode and rewrite the limiting beliefs held deep in my subconscious mind. The process is simple yet profound: you record positive, empowering statements—such as "I am worthy of love" or "My body heals itself with ease"—often set to a background of theta music for the night or alpha music for the day. You then listen to these recordings regularly, allowing the messages to bypass the critical conscious mind and plant new, life-affirming seeds in the fertile ground of your subconscious. Sometimes, I feel as though I am creating a new avatar for myself. While I still occasionally revert to old patterns, I know I just need to keep listening. It is a way of becoming the programmer of your own mind, consciously choosing the internal script that will shape your reality from the inside out.

- **Bodywork**: I love massages and view them as an investment in health. Every other Sunday, we visit Ta, who has healing hands, undoes all the knots in my back, and leaves me feeling relaxed and calm. I could have reflexology every day, as I find it incredibly relaxing and restorative. Unfortunately, the lady who came to our house for years to give us treatments moved to the countryside, and I am still searching for a replacement.

- **Energy Work**: Clearing your chakras is something you cannot see but can learn to feel. When I do not feel grounded or safe in the world, I know I must work on my root chakra. I have also undergone past life regressions, and while the healing is not always immediately obvious, it often takes time to surface.

- **Mind-Body Connection**: Louise Hay taught that every part of the body represents something. Knee and back pain can signify a lack of support, while stomach problems often indicate difficulty digesting life. When I experience pain, I know it is my subconscious mind trying to communicate. The body speaks to you, and if you do not listen, it shouts.

- **Breathing and Grounding**: Breathing is essential. When I cannot sleep, I inhale for a count of seven, hold for four, and exhale for eight; it helps my parasympathetic system relax and soothes my body. Grounding is one of the most accessible therapies. Simply walking barefoot on grass or along the beach can be profoundly healing. I used to teach my students to go outside and ground themselves, and one of them told me that, of all the lessons I had shared, walking barefoot on the grass was something she would always remember.

A Final Thought: The Ultimate Healing Journey

As I write this, I am in a small town in Hungary. Three years ago, my husband suffered a major stroke that left him paralysed on one side. His sister, Carlotta, encouraged him to tap all the parts of his body that he could not feel so that the brain would begin to recognise them. He did this with all his strength while in the hospital. Through his incredible willpower, that practice, and the guidance of a marvellous neuro-physiotherapist, he has made an almost full recovery. We are now at her clinic, where he receives four hours of physiotherapy a day.

In the mornings, I visit the nearby thermal waters. The water is brown and has a peculiar smell, but I have read that it is rich in minerals. The water is 39 degrees, while the air is only 4 degrees, creating magical steam that rises into the cold air. As I float, surrounded by others on their own healing journeys, I visualise my body swimming in minerals, which gives me a profound sense of well-being. This journey is a testament to the power of combining travel, therapy, and a deep, unwavering belief in the body's ability to heal. This type of holiday is the most beneficial experience one can gift to oneself.

Your Wisdom to Go

This week's invitation: Try these three simple practices to explore new ways of resetting your body and mind.

1. **Plan a "Mini-Retreat":** Set aside three hours this weekend. Turn off your phone and do something restorative: take a long bath, read a book, or sit in nature.

2. **Practice Conscious Breathing:** Once a day for the next three days, pause and take five deep, intentional breaths. Place a hand on your belly and feel it expand and contract.

3. **Bring a Lesson Home:** Reflect on a place you have travelled to. What is one quality or custom from that place that you admire? How could you bring a small piece of that energy into your life this week?

Your Journal Prompts

An invitation for reflection: Take a few quiet moments to ponder these questions.

1. What is one "magical moment" you would love to create or experience this year? What is one small step you could take this week to move towards it?

2. Think of a trip or journey that taught you a profound lesson. What was the destination, and what wisdom did you bring home with you?

3. Your body is speaking to you right now. If you close your eyes and listen, is it whispering or shouting? What is the main message it wants you to hear?

Chapter 6

Creating a Healing Environment: Your Home as a Sanctuary

For many years, I saw my home as a collection of things, a place to store my belongings and sleep at night. It was a backdrop to my life, but not an active participant in it. What I have come to understand on my wellness journey is that our environments are not passive. They are living, breathing extensions of ourselves. Our homes are not just containers for our lives; they are powerful creators of our well-being.

Your external world is a mirror of your internal world. When your home is cluttered, chaotic, and filled with things that do not bring you joy, it often reflects a cluttered, chaotic mind. Conversely, when you consciously create a home that is a sanctuary, a space that is clean, calm, beautiful, and filled with intention, you are sending a powerful message to your subconscious mind: I am worthy of peace. I am worthy of beauty. I am worthy of this sanctuary. This chapter is about the practical magic of transforming your home from a simple dwelling to a powerful engine for your well-being.

The Burden of Belongings: Decluttering Your Past

Everything in your home carries an energy. It is imbued with memories, emotions, and the energetic imprint of its history. Some objects have belonged to other people and carry their energy, which can influence what is attracted into our homes. This is why decluttering is one of the most profound spiritual practices you can undertake. It is not just about tidying up; it is about releasing the past and clearing stagnant energy.

I have a tendency to hoard things, a trait I believe is the result of growing up with scarce resources. A cluttered house, however, is a cluttered mind. Since retiring, I have been on a slow and steady mission to declutter. My secret has been to transform this from a daunting project into a gentle daily ritual. Each day, I tidy or clean a small area so that it never becomes an overwhelming task. This consistency prevents burnout and, gradually and peacefully, reclaims my space.

Just as we clean our homes physically, we must also cleanse them energetically. I have learned to clear the energy of the house using sage or Palo Santo, particularly during seasonal changes or after illness has been present in the home.

Creating Flow and Peace: Practical Wisdom

A core principle of a peaceful home is that everything should have a place. Creating order in our external world fosters peace in our internal world. According to Feng Shui expert Marie Diamond, it is essential to keep entryways clear, as the front door is where energy enters the home.

The bedroom, a place of rest and restoration, requires special attention. Beds and wardrobes accumulate stagnant energy, so it is advisable to clear them regularly and never store work-related items under the bed. Ideally, the bed should be positioned so that you face the door while sleeping. Artwork should be calming and romantic. Crucially, mirrors should not be placed directly opposite the bed, as they can disrupt sleep by reflecting energy.

Your Sacred Corner: The Power of an Altar

Creating a sanctuary can begin with one small, sacred corner. I have an altar in my bedroom, a dedicated space that serves as a physical anchor for my intentions. On it, I keep the only photograph I have of myself as a young child, reminding me to nurture my inner child. I also have a collection of stones, rose quartz for love and amethyst for protection, along with inspirational quotes.

Your own sacred space does not need to be elaborate. What matters most is that it contains objects that inspire and ground you. I also keep three sets of oracle cards, which I draw on Monday mornings, or whenever I remember. This practice helps me reflect and set intentions for the days ahead.

Designing for Joy: A Sanctuary for the Senses

We are multi-sensory beings, and our environment profoundly impacts our nervous system. A true sanctuary engages and soothes all our senses.

- **Sight:** Surround yourself with beauty. I have always loved yellow, as it represents light and sunshine. My kitchen is filled with it, and it makes me feel as though the sun is always shining.

- **Sound:** I love to play calming music. Silence, too, is a powerful and healing element of a genuine sanctuary.

- **Smell:** I use essential oils such as lavender in the bedroom to promote calm, and lemon or orange in the kitchen for an uplifting energy. I no longer use candles, as I learnt they can be toxic, particularly for cats. I also prefer not to risk setting my house on fire.

- **Touch:** I believe the two most important pieces of furniture in a home are the bed and the sofa. Investing in their comfort is an investment in your well-being.

- **Taste:** The kitchen is the true heart of the home, a place of joy where we perform the sacred act of creating nourishment. I always keep a bowl of fruit on the counter. I have also started hiding less healthy snacks so they are not constantly tempting me. If I do have a craving, I have to search for them, which often discourages me from indulging.

I have come to believe that your environment reflects what is happening in your mind. This is the key. Tidying your home is a way of tidying your inner world.

A Final Thought: A Sanctuary for Life

Last year, I visited a client of my husband who lived in a huge mansion overlooking the sea. It was the kind of place people dream about. Yet the wife confided that the house was taking over their lives. It made me appreciate my own home even more, because it is cosy, welcoming, and easy to care for.

Your home should be your sanctuary, not your burden. It is not a place to hide from the world, but rather your sacred recharging station. It is the one place on earth where you can feel completely safe and nurtured, allowing you to gather the strength and clarity needed to engage with the world from a place of love and resilience.

In our modern world, this concept extends beyond our physical homes. We can also cultivate virtual sanctuaries. For me, the most powerful example is my Lifebook accountability group. Somehow, the universe brought the four of us together: Jose from Spain, living in Romania; Carolina from Colombia, living in the south of France; Sean from England, living in Brighton; and me from Spain, living in London. For more than four years, we have met almost every week on a video call. It is a sacred, intentional space where we state our goals, share our struggles, and hold one another within a container of support and belief. It is energetically clean, uplifting, and safe. This is a modern sanctuary, demonstrating that the principles of creating a healing environment, intention, safety, and positive energy can be applied to all areas of our lives, both physical and digital.

A Vision for the Future of Home

I envision a world in which our concept of home is completely transformed, becoming the ultimate retreat and the foundation of our well-being. In this future, we all have homes with some land where we can grow our own vegetables, reconnecting us with the earth and the source of our nourishment. The houses themselves are eco-friendly and intelligently designed to protect us from heat and cold with minimal environmental impact. Water is recycled, treated as the precious resource it is, and reused to nourish the gardens that sustain us.

Each person places their own personal stamp on their home, decorating it with natural materials and consciously shaping it into a true sanctuary for rest, creativity, and family time. Most importantly, these homes are part of small, supportive communities where people help and support one another like an extended family, sharing their harvests, their skills, and their lives. This is not simply a vision of a different way of living; it is a return to a more natural, connected, and sustainable way of being.

Your Wisdom to Go

This week's invitation: Begin transforming your relationship with your home through these three simple and intentional practices.

1. **The One-Thing Declutter:** Choose one small area of your home that feels heavy. Spend just 15 minutes clearing it. Release anything that no longer feels joyful or useful. Notice how this small act shifts the energy of the entire room.

2. **Create a Sacred Corner:** Find one small surface in your home and clear it completely. Place one or two objects there that feel beautiful and meaningful to you. Visit this corner once a day for a week and take a slow, deep breath.

3. **Invite in Nature:** Bring one element of nature into your home. This could be a small potted plant, a single flower in a vase, or simply opening the windows to let in fresh air for ten minutes.

Your Journal Prompts

-   **An invitation for reflection:** Take a few quiet moments to consider these questions.

1. How does your home feel to you right now, in one word? How would you like it to feel?

2. If you had to let go of one category of objects from your past, which would it be? What story or identity are you afraid of losing along with it?

3. What is the most sacred space in your home? What makes it feel that way? How could you bring some of that sacred energy into the other rooms of your house?

Part II

The Inner World: Cultivating the Unseen Forces of Well-being

Having built a strong foundation in the tangible world, we now turn our attention inward. The most profound and lasting wellness comes not just from what we do, but from who we are becoming. This second part of our journey is dedicated to the unseen yet powerful forces that shape our reality from the inside out: our thoughts, our feelings, our energy, and our connection to something greater than ourselves. This is sacred inner work. It is the path to reclaiming your personal power, shifting from a victim of circumstance to the conscious creator of your reality. It requires courage, consistency, and gentleness, but it is here, in the quiet landscape of our own hearts, that we find the true source of lasting peace and joy.

Some readers may not identify with, or find this part of the book useful at this moment, and that is perfectly okay, as we are all on different paths. Lately, it seems to me that if we do not see eye to eye with someone, we can begin to see them as enemies, but that should not be the case. Throughout history, we have always thought in different ways, yet we have still coexisted, and that needs to continue. If Part Two of this book feels too far removed for you right now, that is fine. Perhaps you can simply browse it to see if anything resonates, and if it does not, you may choose to return to it at a later date.

In my forties, I was not even aware that a spiritual life existed, and I am pleased that so many young people today are turning to spirituality and talking about trusting the universe. In a world that can often seem frightening, our inner world, if we cultivate it, can become a place of refuge when everything else fails or no longer makes sense.

Happiness is a choice we make every day, every hour, every minute. Cultivating an inner world gives us hope, which is also a discipline. Instead of being drawn into negativity, with consistency and persistence, we can develop a positive outlook on life that makes our lives more bearable and even joyful. For this reason, I believe we should limit how much news we consume, because when we watch too much of it, we can start to feel as though the world is coming to an end.

This second part is also an act of courage on my part, as I know I expose myself to being misunderstood, judged, and criticised. The only thing I ask is that you approach it with an open mind, both towards me and towards the world. One of our greatest challenges today is learning how not to agree with someone while still respecting their views.

This inward journey, however, is not a retreat from the world; it is one of the most powerful ways to prepare ourselves to engage with it. When we improve ourselves, we are better equipped to improve the world. Working on ourselves is the best way to awaken everything within us and around us. This is the promise of the chapters that follow.

The only thing I can do for you is to work on myself, the only thing you can do for me is to work on yourself.

Chapter 7

Self-Love and Self-Care: The Foundation of Everything

For many years, if you had asked me about self-love, I would have thought it meant getting a massage or buying a new scarf. Like so many of us, I used to confuse self-care with self-love. Self-care is about the things we do to make ourselves feel better; it is an external practice. Self-love is the feeling we hold for ourselves deep within; it is an internal experience. It can be compared to the unconditional love we feel for our children or our pets. While self-care can certainly help us feel more loved, the real work, and the most profound and challenging work, is cultivating a deep and abiding sense of self-worth that does not depend on any external action.

This is a practice I have been trying to deepen, observe, and understand for many years. I have discovered that it is one of the most difficult things to put into practice, because the roots of our self-worth do not lie in our conscious mind, but deep within our subconscious. Like most people, my subconscious carried the belief that I was not good enough and that I did not belong. This chapter is about the journey of learning how to rewrite that story.

The Oxygen Mask Principle: Putting Yourself First

The idea of putting yourself first can seem selfish in a world that often teaches us to be selfless. Yet consider the safety instructions on an aeroplane: we are always told to put on our own oxygen mask before helping our children. Why? Because if we run out of oxygen, we are of no use to anyone.

This is the essence of true self-love. I have observed that within a family, when the mother has healthy self-esteem, she can extend that stability to the rest of the family. She becomes a grounding presence who can create harmony around her. We must take care of ourselves so we can care for others.

The Practice of Self-Care: Actions That Nurture the Soul

While self-love is the goal, acts of self-care are the practical steps that help us reach it. Each act of care sends a powerful message to the subconscious: I am worthy of beauty, comfort, and joy.

We are multi-sensory beings, and we must approach self-love in the same way we approach well-being, from all angles and through all our senses. This practice can take many forms:

- **For the eyes:** Surrounding myself with beauty, whether that means wearing a beautiful scarf or choosing a café with lovely décor. A particularly liberating decision I made at the age of fifty was to stop wearing high heels, as comfort became my priority.
- **For the ears:** Playing music while doing housework or driving, to lift my mood and raise my energy. Listening to inspirational podcasts and continuing to learn every day.
- **For the nose:** Using a diffuser with essential oils such as lavender or tea tree to help me feel relaxed, happy, and grounded. Smelling the flowers in my garden or while walking in a park.

Self-care also involves learning the power of saying no, which I still find difficult, although I often try to offer an alternative. For example, I might say, "I cannot go for a walk with you today, but perhaps we could try next week."

Equally important is the right to change your mind. We often feel guilty when we need to rearrange plans or adopt a different outlook, but we should not be harsh with ourselves. Changing our minds is a sign of growth and of honouring the person we are today, not the person we were yesterday.

The Inner Work: Becoming Your Own Ally

Ultimately, no amount of beautiful shoes or skilfully navigated conversations can replace the inner work required to cultivate genuine self-love. This work takes place in the quiet space of our own minds.

Our minds are naturally trained to focus on the negative. Our brains tend to cling to negative experiences while letting positive ones slip away. This is why our internal dialogue is so important. For most of my life, my self-talk was predominantly negative. We often speak to ourselves in ways we would never speak to our worst enemy. Learning to change this pattern requires constant, conscious awareness. It is the practice of becoming your own greatest ally instead of your harshest critic.

A central part of this process is learning to work with the subconscious. One exercise I learned from Louise Hay may sound silly, yet it truly works. Stand in front of the mirror and say, "Lu, I love you. I really, really love you." When I remember to practise this consistently, I feel a noticeable shift. I choose to send love instead of criticism, trusting that I am a magnet for what I wish to attract into my life.

For empaths, this inner work also includes learning how to protect oneself. A deeply liberating realisation is understanding that you are not responsible for other people. When I finally integrated this belief, I felt an immense sense of freedom. I now understand that we are here to accompany one another, but that each of us must walk our own path.

A Final Thought: The One You Have Been Waiting For

Self-love is not a destination; it is a journey. Perfection does not exist; it is merely an ideal. One way I know that I do not yet fully love myself is that, after twenty years of studying nutrition, I still occasionally eat foods that upset my stomach, such as sugar or gluten. When this happens, I tell myself it is like a vaccination; if I never consume them, I might become intolerant. Yet it is also a reminder that I am, and will always be, a work in progress, and I have learned to accept that.

When you truly love yourself, you radiate from within. You attract people who appreciate your energy and resonate at a similar level. You become magnetic, and instead of hoping for things to happen, you live with the deep knowing that whatever unfolds will be for your highest good.

Remember this powerful truth: "You are the one you have been waiting for." This statement is profoundly empowering because it encourages self-reliance and personal responsibility for your own destiny. It is an invitation to step out of victimhood, to stop blaming others, and to begin creating the life you desire from a place of deep, unconditional self-love.

A Vision for the Future of Self-Love

I envision a future in which we become wiser, where self-love is not something we must relearn in adulthood, but a quality we embody naturally from the moment we are born. In this future, parents will instinctively know how to raise their children in ways that help them cultivate a positive, supportive, and loving internal dialogue from their earliest years. Self-care will no longer be seen as an indulgence, but as a normal and essential part of daily life, as natural as breathing. As our collective consciousness evolves, new and innovative approaches to relaxation and self-care will emerge, helping us to nurture our inner world with increasing grace and ease. This is the ultimate foundation for a healthier world: a world in which every child grows up knowing, without doubt, that they are worthy of their own love.

Your Wisdom to Go

This week's invitation: Try these three simple practices to begin building a deeper foundation of self-love.

1. **The Mirror Challenge:** For the next three days, first thing in the morning, look yourself in the eyes in the mirror. Place a hand on your heart, say your name, and say, "I love you." Hold your gaze for ten seconds and simply notice how it feels.

2. **Conduct a "Fun Audit":** Ask yourself, "How can I make this more fun?" Choose one routine task and intentionally add an element of pleasure, such as your favourite music, a podcast, or an essential oil.

3. **Practise the Empowered No:** The next time someone asks you to do something you do not have the time or energy for, practise saying no kindly but

firmly. Try this phrase: "Thank you so much for asking, but I cannot make that work right now."

Your Journal Prompts

An invitation to reflect: Take a few quiet moments to consider the following questions.

1. What is the main message your inner critic tells you? If you were to give that voice a name, what would it be? What is one loving truth you could offer in response?

2. What is one "outside job." an act of self-care, that you could do this week to make your "inside job," your sense of self-love, a little easier?

3. Think of a recent time when you said "yes" but wanted to say "no." What were you afraid might happen? What is one small, low-risk "no" you could practise saying this week?

Chapter 8

Meditation: Becoming Familiar with Yourself

Again, meditation is one of those things that, when practised regularly, enhances well-being. Yet few people have the discipline to maintain a consistent practice. I have tried all sorts of meditation and, after a while, I tend to give up. I know that when I do meditate, I feel calmer and more connected, but like sleep, meditation remains something of a mystery to me.

Meditation is the deliberate focusing of attention to cultivate calm and heightened awareness. According to Dr Joe Dispenza, meditation means to "become familiar with." I understand this as becoming familiar with oneself and with one's recurring thoughts. For me, it is also a tool for conscious creation. Before I go to bed, I ask myself how I have done that day. When I wake up, I try to meditate on the day ahead by reflecting on what I want to do and, more importantly, how I want to feel and who I want to be.

Finding a Practice That Fits

For years, I believed meditation had to be done sitting bolt upright in uncomfortable silence. I have since learned that the best practice is the one you will actually do. We often think meditation is about switching off the mind and blocking out all thoughts, but that is almost impossible. I believe meditation is about bringing greater awareness to our thought patterns, focusing on the present moment, changing how we relate to our thoughts, slowing our brains, and gaining a deeper understanding of our true selves.

Repeating a mantra is easier for me than observing my thoughts. I also prefer guided meditations, as you can simply listen. The secret is finding someone whose voice resonates with you rather than irritates you. The mind, like the body, needs exercise, but it also craves ease. My favourite meditation teacher, Davidji, says that "comfort is bliss," and I completely agree. That is one of the reasons I used to meditate lying down. When situations or circumstances in our lives are challenging, it can be helpful to stop pushing and instead allow. Let go and attract what you want towards you.

Wisdom in Practice: A Post-Meditation Check-In

After meditating, we can ask ourselves a few gentle questions to deepen our awareness:

- Was I able to keep my eyes closed?
- Was I distracted?
- What was the focus of my mind?
- What did I feel? What did I see?
- How do I feel after meditation?

Deeper Currents: Energy, Frequencies, and the Pineal Gland

In my insatiable quest for self-improvement, I came across Ray Behan, who uses meditation and breath alongside solfeggio frequencies to help people heal. His theory is that we are frequency, and that frequencies can heal us. His seven-chakra meditation gives me a sense of well-being that lasts throughout the day.

This energy work also connects to the physical body. It is said that the pineal gland, situated inside the forehead, is the seat of the soul. It produces melatonin, which is inhibited by light. This is why I refuse to have bright lights on in the evening. The pineal gland can become calcified through the consumption of chlorinated water, so when I used to meditate, I sometimes set the intention to connect with and clear my pineal gland.

Meditation in Motion: Making Your Entire Day a Practice

Lately, I have been playing with the idea of making my entire day a meditation, instead of meditating for twenty minutes every day. This represents a profound shift from viewing meditation as an isolated activity to embracing it as a way of being. Whatever we choose to do must be easily integrated into our daily lives, because otherwise, we are more likely to give up. Resilience and discipline can wear thin, so when something requires sustained effort, there often comes a point where we stop. Our minds desire ease and are wired to seek comfort rather than discomfort.

So, if I am doing the dishes, I focus fully on that task. If I am walking in nature, I look around and absorb the beauty. When I go to the gym, I leave my phone in my locker and concentrate on my body and my movements. This practice is about being fully present in each moment.

The Inner Sanctuary: Finding Silence in a Noisy World

Silence is the ultimate language, one we rarely use because we are constantly surrounded by noise and chatter, both externally and within our own minds. The inner dialogue is relentless and, most of the time, negative. I believe this is one of the main reasons so many of us suffer from anxiety.

We are also continuously bombarded with information, and I am becoming increasingly selective about what I allow into my mind. Lately, I find myself asking more often whether I really need something in my life. I am saying no to more things, and I feel myself becoming a little reclusive. When I was younger, I loved being surrounded by people all the time, perhaps to fill the emptiness that many of us carry inside. After lockdown, or perhaps after turning sixty, I have noticed a significant shift. I no longer want to burden myself with other people's energy or problems. I would rather spend time alone, doing my courses, writing, and enjoying inner peace.

A Vision for the Future of Meditation

My vision for the future of meditation is that, as our lives change and improve, we will no longer need to meditate as a separate activity. Instead, we will have learned to exist in a meditative state all the time. We will live lives of natural mindfulness, instinctively knowing how to be fully present and engaged in whatever we are doing in the moment. In this future, we will master the art of consciously visualising the life we want to create, and this practice will reduce the anxiety that arises from uncertainty. We will also learn to look at the past with wisdom rather than regret, allowing its lessons to inform our future in a powerful and positive way. The ultimate goal of meditation is not to become skilled at meditating, but to become so present, peaceful, and empowered that our entire life becomes a living meditation.

A Final Thought

I have come to the realisation that happiness, or contentment, is something we carry within us and simply need to uncover. There is no point searching for it externally. It already exists inside us, and it is up to us to find it and release it. It is like being in an aeroplane on a cloudy day;

once the plane rises above the clouds, the sun is always there, shining.

A candle loses nothing by lighting another candle. When we shine our light, we illuminate our own lives and the lives of others. I have reached the conclusion that life is about walking steadily in the direction we wish to go. Slowly, we move closer to where we want to be, always remembering that we are on a journey and will never fully arrive. The same is true of meditation.

Can we stop thoughts? Can we live our lives in mindfulness?

Your Wisdom to Go

This week's invitation: Try these three simple practices to integrate meditation into your life.

1. **Find a Resonant Voice:** Explore a guided meditation app, such as Insight Timer or Calm, and listen to three different teachers. Notice whose voice and style help you feel most at ease.

2. **Practise Meditation in Motion:** Choose one daily activity, such as washing dishes or making tea. For that short time, give it your full and undivided attention. Notice the sounds, smells, and sensations.

3. **Schedule a Silence Snack:** Once this week, find five minutes to sit in silence. Do not try to stop your thoughts. Simply notice them without judgment.

Your Journal Prompts

An invitation for reflection: Take a few quiet moments to consider these questions.

1. What is the most common or recurring thought you notice when you quiet your mind?

2. When you feel scattered or overwhelmed, what is one simple thing that always helps you feel more centred and calm?

3. If you were to make your entire day a meditation, what is one activity you could begin with today?

Chapter 9

Feelings, Emotions, and Healing – Learning the Language of Your Soul

For most of my life, I was very afraid of "bad" feelings. Like so many of us, I learned to see emotions as things to be controlled, managed, or ideally avoided altogether. I lived in my head, a place that felt safer and more logical than the unpredictable landscape of my heart. What I have come to understand, however, is that our feelings are not the enemy. They are the language of our soul and the messengers of our deepest truths. To heal is to learn how to listen to them.

This journey requires courage. It means developing the willingness to look at the feelings we have pushed down and to locate them in our bodies. It is not an easy task, but it is the most rewarding work we can ever do. When we learn to develop a healthy relationship with our feelings, we unlock the door to true and lasting inner peace.

Energy in Motion: A New Way to See Your Feelings

The first and most important shift is to let go of the idea of "good" and "bad" emotions. There are no bad emotions.

They are all simply part of the human experience. They are energy, and the word emotion itself can be understood as E-motion, energy in motion.

Think of your emotions like a river. When the river is allowed to flow, it is healthy, vibrant, and full of life. When we build a dam to stop it, when we suppress our anger or numb our sadness, the water becomes stagnant, murky, and toxic. On their own, emotions only last for a minute and a half. It is the story that we attach to them that prevents them from moving on. This is why it is so helpful to say, "I feel angry" instead of "I am angry," as this creates space between you and the feeling.

Problems arise when we do not let the river flow. When we suppress our feelings, that energy becomes trapped in our bodies, where it can manifest as tension, chronic pain, and even illness. I have noticed that when I am consistently living in a state of joy, moments of sadness or anger feel much stronger when they arise. However, the gift is that by setting my default state to positivity, I do not stay down for long.

The Fight or Flight Habit: How Thoughts Create Your Reality

For many years, particularly during my career as a secondary school teacher, the feeling I most identified with was overwhelm. Teachers in this country are heroes, carrying an immense weight on their shoulders. That internal conflict creates a profound and chronic state of stress. I physically developed broad, heavy shoulders, as though I were carrying that weight at all times.

I have since come to realise that my body had been on high alert, locked in a state of fight-or-flight for decades. When we exist in this state, our bodies are continually flooded with the stress hormone cortisol. This state is often triggered and sustained by our own thoughts. Feelings are created by thoughts, and our thoughts can be addictive. This is where our power lies. We become what we think, and it is up to us to choose thoughts that serve us.

It takes four positive emotions to counteract a negative one, which is why we must make a constant and conscious effort to cultivate feelings that uplift us. This is the art of self-regulation, the ability to influence how we want to feel. I have learned that the most effective way to stop worrying is to take action. I make a decision and act on it. This is a powerful way to break the cycle of stressful thinking.

Your Body Is Speaking: Are You Listening?

Our bodies are the keepers of our emotional truths. For years, I held my emotions in my gut, often referred to as our "second brain." To this day, my stomach can still become sore and inflamed from unprocessed feelings. When we feel low, it is as though we are in the basement of a house, while all the resources we need, such as joy, light, and peace, are on the upper floors.

The body is always trying to heal, and it communicates with us through discomfort. If we ignore its whispers, it will eventually shout through pain. It is also important to learn the different languages the body speaks. A gut feeling is often the signal that tells us, "Do not do it!" It is a primal and protective response. Intuition, however, often whispers, "Do it!" It is an expansive, soul-level calling.

The tension between these two signals can leave us feeling unfulfilled, because intuition urges growth while the gut seeks safety. Learning to distinguish between them is a profound practice that can bring a deep sense of well-being.

A Toolkit for Emotional Healing

A long time ago, during a Louise Hay course, I realised that what my soul was truly seeking was not happiness, but inner peace. To protect that inner peace, I am learning to observe the turmoil of the world without absorbing it. Life humbles you. As you grow older, you stop chasing the grand things and begin to value the small ones. Simplicity becomes the ultimate goal.

I have also come to believe that many conditions are "foodable." Most chronic conditions begin with inflammation, which can often be reduced by removing inflammatory foods such as gluten, sugar, and dairy from our diet. Stress is also a major contributor to illness and inflammation, and even emotions have been described as molecules within the body.

Music, too, is a powerful healer. Recently, I have been listening to music with a healing frequency of 7.83 Hz, which is said to align with the Earth's magnetic field.

The most important tool, however, is the belief that we are all capable of healing ourselves. I have been through the dark night of the soul, an experience that I am still not able to write about. It is a place of absolute desolation. Yet what I learned is that even in the deepest darkness, there is a flicker of light within us. Afterwards, we have a choice. We can become a victim, or we can choose to grow. Feeling well is a service to others.

Wisdom in Practice: A Map of Our Deepest Emotions

Certain emotions carry a unique weight and offer distinct lessons on our healing journey:

- **Shame:** Shame carries the lowest emotional frequency. It is the painful belief that we are fundamentally flawed. It thrives in secrecy and silence. The only way to heal shame is to bring it into the light, to share our story with a trusted friend and realise that we are not alone.

- **Courage:** Courage is not the absence of fear. One of my latest discoveries is that the body cannot distinguish between fear and excitement. When I feel fearful, I tell myself that I am excited, and this reframing gives me the courage to move forward. It is a way of transforming energy and taking brave action. It is the energy that lifts you out of the basement.

- **Fear:** Of all emotions, my relationship with fear has been the most challenging. Growing up in Spain under Franco's dictatorship, combined with the strictures of the Catholic religion, conditioned me to live in a constant state of fear, a feeling I still carry with me today. It is an old and familiar companion.

I have come to understand that fear and worry are, at their core, forms of negative manifestation. They involve cultivating the very experiences we wish to avoid. As my cousin Angel wisely says, to worry is to "occupy yourself before it is time." I am learning to welcome fear when it arises, to observe it, to thank it for attempting to protect me, and to consciously transmute its energy into courage or excitement. This is a deep and demanding practice, because this feeling is not confined to my thoughts. It feels etched into my very DNA, an echo of the past that still whispers its warnings.

People who live in fear react rather than respond, and that is something I am determined not to do. Fear and worry are like paying interest on money we have not yet borrowed.

A Vision for the Future of Healing

My dream for the future of healing is that we will learn to cultivate a beautiful and powerful relationship with our inner world. In this future, we will learn to acknowledge and accept all our emotions, understanding that they are not enemies to be suppressed, but a compass that guides us through life. We will master the art of self-regulation, allowing feelings to move through us without becoming stuck, and using their energy and wisdom to inform our choices. As we do this, we will unlock the profound, innate power of the body to heal itself, recognising that much of our physical illness is simply the result of unprocessed emotional energy. We will become deeply connected to our own energy, and we will learn how to harness it, not only for our own benefit, but to bring about what will make life better for the whole human race. This is the ultimate healing: transforming our pain into power, and our feelings into fuel for a better world.

A Final Thought: Learning to Be Your Own Observer

In our modern world, we often place great value on intellectual intelligence, but I have come to believe that the key to a truly successful and fulfilling life lies in something far deeper: emotional intelligence. It is far more than simply managing our feelings. I see it as the ultimate art of well-being. It is the profound ability to understand, navigate, and harness the power of your inner world, your thoughts, feelings, and intuition, in such a way that you can consciously influence the world outside you. When you develop emotional intelligence, you no longer react to life from a place of old wounds or unconscious patterns. Instead, you learn to respond with wisdom, compassion, and intention. You become the alchemist of your own experience, capable of transforming moments of challenge into opportunities for growth, and your own inner peace into a calming presence that positively affects everyone you meet. This is the true power we all hold: the power to use our inner world to create a better outer world.

Healing from our emotional past is a lifelong journey. Having been sent to boarding school at the age of seven, I carried deep abandonment issues that led me into many toxic relationships. Why was I not taught about boundaries? I had to learn the hard way. For a long time, I lost my *joie de vivre*, my authentic self buried beneath layers of roles I played to keep the peace.

Now, I am learning to become my own observer. This is how we begin to forge our character. Character is not our personality; it is something we practise. We are the sculptors of our lives, and in moments of conscious choice, we take responsibility for the person we are becoming. It involves developing the awareness to notice when I am angry, sad, or frustrated, and allowing those energies to move through me without becoming stuck. Part of this observation is also recognising that some emotions are not our own. As an empath, I am learning about enmeshment, the unconscious taking on of other people's feelings. A crucial question then becomes, "Is this feeling even mine?" This is the bravest work we can do.

Your Wisdom to Go

This week's invitation: try these three simple practices to begin healing your relationship with your emotions.

1. **Locate the Feeling:** The next time you experience a strong emotion, close your eyes. Instead of getting lost in the story, ask yourself, "Where does this live in my body?" Place your hand on that area and breathe into it for 30 seconds.

2. **Interrupt the Pattern:** When you notice yourself caught in a loop of negative thinking, interrupt the pattern with a physical action. Stand up, stretch your arms towards the sky, or step outside for a breath of fresh air.

3. **Find Your Inner Peace Anchor:** Identify one simple thing that consistently brings you a sense of inner peace, such as a song, a photograph, or a memory. When you feel overwhelmed, intentionally bring this anchor to mind for one minute.

Your Journal Prompts

An invitation for reflection: take a few quiet moments to consider these questions.

1. Think of a "difficult" emotion you tend to avoid. What is your greatest fear about what might happen if you allowed yourself to truly feel it?

2. Describe a time when you felt completely overwhelmed. Where did you feel that "heavyweight" in your body? What is one thing you could have done in that moment to offer yourself a small measure of compassion?

3. What does "inner peace" feel like in your body? Is it warm or cool, still or flowing? Describe the physical sensation of your own inner peace.

Chapter 10

Spirituality, Energy, and Life – Connecting to Something More

Spirituality, for me, is not something I was aware of in my youth; it is something I have developed later in life. I remember one day when my lovely friend Nathalie, whom I met while studying nutrition, told me, "You need a spiritual life," and just like that, I began searching. For those of us who are seekers, there is no stopping. It is not about religion, although I was brought up Catholic and lost my faith along the way. Spirituality is a connection with something greater than oneself, our true self, our higher self, the universe, or whatever name resonates with you. I have also realised that spirituality is about imagining and believing that everything is possible, and that brings me an enormous sense of well-being. It is the feeling that we are all connected, that we are all one, and that we are, in essence, part of a divine energy. We are the waves, and at the same time, we are the ocean. This understanding has been the greatest gift of my journey. Spirituality is about imagining and believing that everything is possible, and that is a beautiful thought.

For those of you who might be sceptical, I offer this gentle reflection: this is not about rigid belief, but about personal experience. Sometimes it is not about believing something, but about allowing yourself to enjoy the possibility of it. If a message in this chapter does not resonate with you, you can simply set it aside.

I feel, at this moment, that there is a collective awakening occurring on our planet. The thought that we are co-creators of a more beautiful world fills me with hope. One of the most grounding spiritual practices in my life is my weekly study of *A Course in Miracles* with my dear friends Sylvie and Milena. The main message of the book is that when we are in our ego, we suffer. The book itself is extraordinarily complex and can take years to master, but gradually, the messages of unconditional love seep through, and you begin to see life in a more beautiful and forgiving way. It helps you to refrain from judgment and brings a profound sense of joy. I regard this weekly meeting as a beautiful spiritual practice, a sacred appointment that helps us avoid unconscious habits and ensures we reflect. It is like mental training that helps reshape your thinking so that you see everything with love. It trains both mind and body to avoid falling into emotions that do not serve you, and it is, for me, a consistent and gentle way to find peace, understanding, and true wellness.

The Nature of Energy: The Unseen Force

At its core, a spiritual life is the recognition that everything is energy. I believe that everything, even money, is a form of energy. To attract it, you must feel that you deserve it. You have to allow it, welcome it, and circulate it with joy and generosity. When I spend money, I think of it as spreading good and abundance.

This is especially true of people. They can either recharge you like a battery or drain your energy. I always pay attention to how I feel after spending time with someone. According to research by David Hawkins, "One individual who vibrates to the energy of pure love will counterbalance the negativity of 750,000 who do not." In a world gone mad, the greatest revolution is to return to love.

The best way I have found to recharge is to connect with nature. When I feel tired or sad, I sit among the trees, or even near a plant, and open my hands with the intention of recharging. The most powerful energy of all is the sun. Whenever it shines, I am out there like a battery, soaking it in. The sun nourishes both my body and my soul. Even in recent summers in Spain, when the sun felt so strong that it was almost abrasive, I still embraced it.

Your Personal Energy Field: Home, Light, and the Shadow

This unseen energy is not just "out there"; it exists in our homes, in our bodies, and in our hearts. Electricity is another form of energy that enhances our lives, but like everything else, it must be used wisely. I have learned to keep the lights dim in the evening; otherwise, the body will not begin producing melatonin, which aids sleep.

Colours can also influence how we feel, as each chakra is associated with a colour. Many years ago, my lovely friend Aneta conducted a colour analysis for me and recommended that I wear strong colours. I always follow this advice, as it lifts my spirits. I love yellow, which, for me, represents light and sun. I have chosen fuchsia as my personal colour to remind me to be Lu, and when I wear my vibrant fuchsia coat, people often tell me that it cheers them up.

We are also like mirrors. What we perceive in others, especially qualities we dislike, it often reflects a part of our own shadow self. In my quest for self-understanding, I strive to embrace all aspects of myself. I make a point of being aware of the energy I carry. I would like to think that I am a torch of light and love. I believe in the power of intention, which provides the frequency needed to attract what we desire. Our frequency is like our currency.

The energy of our intention is focused and amplified through our words. Ancient traditions have always revered the power of the spoken word, using chants, prayers, and incantations. The famous magical phrase Abracadabra is not merely a relic of fairy tales; in ancient Hebrew, it translates as "As I speak, I create." This is the profound secret of manifestation. We must be mindful of how we speak because our words are not just descriptions of reality; they are the tools we use to shape it. Every thought we think, every emotion we feel, and every word we utter is a command sent into the world. Our subconscious mind, our soul, and the universe are always listening, working together to manifest the energy we project. If we speak of lack, we create lack. If we speak of gratitude and possibility, we create a life that mirrors that beautiful frequency. This is not just a spiritual belief; it is the deepest form of personal responsibility.

Deeper Currents: Chakras, Past Lives, and Unseen Support

Our bodies are surrounded by energy fields known as chakras. When they are open and unblocked, I feel that I can flow with life. We have seven chakras:

1. **The Root Chakra:** Located at the perineum, it grounds us. When blocked, we may feel unsafe and disconnected from our body.

2. **The Sacral Chakra:** Enhances creativity. When blocked, we may feel low in energy or experience a lack of creative inspiration.

3. **The Solar Plexus Chakra:** Fuels self-esteem. When blocked, we may experience digestive issues and feel powerless.

4. **The Heart Chakra:** Governs love and compassion. When blocked, we may feel unloved and bitter.

5. **The Throat Chakra:** Connected to self-expression. When blocked, we may suppress our feelings, which can lead to weight gain or illness.

6. **The Third Eye Chakra:** Enhances intuition. When blocked, we may feel lost or experience headaches.

7. **The Crown Chakra:** Connects us to the universe. When blocked, we may feel spiritually disconnected and cynical.

This understanding naturally leads to a belief in past lives. Since we are energy, and energy only transforms, it makes sense that our soul continues to exist after the body ceases. I believe the white butterflies I often see are the spirits of my mum, dad, or brothers coming to greet me. They are a constant reminder that we are never alone. I believe we have a team of unseen support—our ancestors, our angels, our inner wisdom. But, as the angel expert Kyle Gray says, we must ask for their guidance.

Wisdom in Practice: A Simple Prayer for Trusting the Universe

When you find yourself in a challenging situation, ask for help with this simple, powerful prayer:

"Please help me resolve this situation for the highest good of all involved."

Wisdom in Practice: Choosing Your Lucky Sign

We can all invite a little more magic into our lives by choosing a personal lucky sign. For me, that sign has always been the butterfly. It is the ultimate symbol of transformation, the miraculous journey from a humble caterpillar into a being of flight and beauty. It is a constant reminder that profound change is always possible. For this reason, the butterfly graces the cover of this book. I see them everywhere, especially the white butterflies, which I believe are the spirits of my brothers coming to greet me. Their presence always fills me with a sense of peace and joy. People who regularly walk with me can testify that this is true. I have them scattered throughout my house and garden.

I invite you to choose your own lucky sign, something that, whenever you see it, brings you a spark of joy, luck, and inspiration. It could be a feather, a specific number sequence such as 11:11, a robin, or a rainbow. It does not matter what it is, only that it feels special to you. Let it be your personal wink from the universe, a confirmation that you are on the right path, and a beautiful reminder of your own capacity for transformation.

Finding Your Purpose: A Life of Meaning

Life itself is a master teacher, but its most profound lessons often arise from our deepest sorrows. After losing two brothers, one at 53 and the other at 62, and experiencing a grief that reshaped my world, I came to understand that life always presents us with a choice. When bad things happen, you can either become a victim or choose to become stronger. I chose to grow. For me, this meant learning the art of living. It was no longer enough to simply exist or plan for a distant future; I had to learn how to find and create joy in the present.

This is when I began consciously collecting what I call *'polaroid moments'*—those beautiful, magical times when life feels full and vibrant. When I am enjoying myself or in a truly beautiful place, I mentally capture the moment, so that when days are grey or uneventful, I have a library of light to draw from, a tangible reminder that magical days are always coming.

We all ask ourselves at some point: What is the purpose of our lives? I believe we are here to learn, evolve, be happy, and be of service. I was told that I was the chosen one in my family to evolve and break patterns. I believe that our generation is here to heal past generations. This reframes our personal healing journey not as a selfish act, but as a sacred responsibility.

For me, purpose is not found in a grand title, but in the small, sacred moments of connection. The answers are the breadcrumbs that will lead you home to a life of meaning.

A Vision for the Future of Life's Final Transition

I envision a future where our understanding of life expands so profoundly that we no longer fear its end. In this future, we will not fear death because we will understand that it is not a finality but simply a transition. We will know, with deep and unshakable certainty, that we are eternal beings of energy, and that what we call "death" is merely the act of stepping from this reality into a parallel world. This understanding will transform our lives, freeing us from the anxiety of endings and allowing us to live more fully, bravely, and joyfully in the present, secure in the knowledge that our journey never truly ceases—it simply changes form.

A Vision for the Future of Spirituality

In my ideal vision for the future, spirituality will not be something we discover late in life; it will be an intrinsic part of our being, to which we are all connected from the moment we are born. In this future, we will instinctively use our spirituality to harness the energy of our lives, allowing it to guide us into constant connection with our Higher Selves. We will learn to communicate routinely with our masters, guides, and our own inner wisdom, seeking their counsel in our daily lives as a normal and natural practice. We will walk through the world with a deep, unshakable knowing that we are always protected and supported by our ancestors and angels. This is not a future of seeking, but of knowing; a future where every soul is born already connected to the divine light within.

A Final Thought: Change Your Energy, Change Your Life

As we grow older, we learn not to care so much about what others think. It is then that the most important relationship can truly begin: the one with yourself. When you find the energy to start loving yourself, you become a powerful force that attracts better experiences. You change your energy, and you change your life. We are all just energy, passing through. The question is, what legacy do we want to leave behind?

Your Wisdom to Go

This week's invitation: try these three simple practices to connect with the subtle energy in and around you.

1. **Conduct a Personal Energy Audit:** For one day, pay close attention to how you feel after interacting with different people and activities. At the end of the day, write down one thing that recharged you and one thing that drained you.

2. **Practice a Chakra Affirmation:** Place your hand gently over your throat. Take three deep breaths. On the last exhale, say aloud: "I express what is in my heart with ease and clarity."

3. **Ask for Help:** The next time you face a small, frustrating challenge, try the prayer: "Please help me resolve this for the highest good."

Your Journal Prompts

An invitation for reflection: take a few quiet moments to ponder these questions.

1. Think of a person who really triggers you. What specific quality in them irritates you the most? Now, gently ask yourself: "Where does a small part of that same quality live in me?"

2. What is your "white butterfly"? Is there a sign or symbol that always feels like a message from the universe or a loved one?

3. If you truly believed you had a team of unseen supporters waiting to help you, what is the one thing you would ask for help with right now?

Chapter 11

The Second Spring: Navigating Menopause with Power and Grace

There is a season in every woman's life that our culture rarely speaks of with reverence. It is framed as an ending, a loss, a slow fade into irrelevance. I am speaking of menopause. For years, I approached it with a sense of dread, armed only with the frightening stories of my mother's generation. What I have come to discover, however, is that this narrative is not only incomplete; it is profoundly untrue.

This transition is not an ending. It is an initiation. In Chinese medicine, this stage of life is referred to as the "Second Spring," a time when a woman's energy, no longer directed outward towards creating and nurturing others, turns inward to cultivate her own deepest wisdom. I was told that in the old days, people believed that after a woman stopped menstruating, the blood would go to her head, making her wiser and more intuitive, which I admire. It is a powerful call to come home to yourself.

My journey to Japan offered me not only lessons in grace and intention but also a profound new perspective on life's transitions. I was fascinated to learn that in Japan, menopause is known as *Kōnenki*, a term that translates more closely to "renewal years" or "climacteric years." The language itself reframes the experience, suggesting a gradual, natural process rather than an abrupt and final "pause." It is not viewed as a medical problem to be aggressively "fixed," but as a natural, albeit sometimes challenging, stage of a woman's life. Interestingly, Japanese women have historically reported fewer of the classic Western symptoms, such as hot flashes, a difference many researchers attribute to their traditional diet, rich in natural phytoestrogens found in soy. The cultural approach is one of quiet grace, patience, and endurance. This offered me a powerful new lens through which to view my own journey, a reminder that our experience of menopause is profoundly shaped by our culture, our diet, and our mindset, and that it can be navigated not as a crisis, but as a natural part of life.

But this homecoming is not a passive event. It is a journey that demands our full attention. I was fortunate to be able to retire from my working life when I did, because deep in my soul, I knew that my body would not be able to handle the added stress of menopause on top of my demanding career. It is as if your soul finally says, "Enough of this. You have not come here to do things that are not aligned with who you are." This chapter is about learning to step up and honour that call.

Your Body is Speaking a New Language: The Physical Shift

The most undeniable change for many women is what happens to the body. It can feel like a betrayal when, despite eating and exercising as you always have, you begin to put on weight, especially around the middle. As oestrogen production declines, our metabolism slows, and our bodies tend to store fat more readily. The loss of oestrogen affects us in numerous ways: it disrupts our sleep, contributes to weight gain, anxiety, and depression.

The truth is, nowadays we are exposed to so many chemicals and microplastics that we need to support our hormones in ways our ancestors never had to. This is the first place we are asked to "step up." Our bodies are requesting a new kind of support. In menopause, women need to rest more, address their traumas, adjust their exercise routines, and take a proactive approach with nutrition and supplementation.

A Toolkit for Thriving: The Art of Self-Experimentation

Balancing hormones is a complex topic, and the journey of menopause is the ultimate lesson in becoming your own best expert. You are not looking for a single magic bullet; you are slowly, patiently building an arsenal of tools that work for you. At times, it can feel overwhelming, as though one symptom follows another: sudden pains and aches, thinning eyebrows, memory lapses, disrupted sleep, despite your best efforts. The list could go on, but it is best not to dwell on it.

For many, the first consideration is Hormone Replacement Therapy (HRT). I have found that the decision is very personal and should be made with a doctor. Because I do not wish to use hormonal therapy, I have found other ways to support my body. I use a wild yam cream by Barbara O'Neill when I remember. I cannot prove that it helps, but the simple, loving act of applying it is a powerful placebo that makes me feel better. I have also adopted seed cycling and take a high-quality Omega-3 supplement, which has significantly helped alleviate the aches and pains in my body.

Wisdom in Practice: The Holistic View of a "Damp" Body

From a Chinese medicine perspective, during my menopausal journey, I was told that my body was showing signs of "dampness"—an internal environment of sluggishness that can manifest as bloating and weight gain. The prescription was simple yet profound: avoid cold and raw foods. According to this wisdom, a "damp" system lacks the internal "fire" to properly digest cold foods. Eating warming foods helps to reduce the dampness and restore balance. It is also recommended to start the day with warm water infused with ginger and cinnamon to help bring heat into the body.

Building a Resilient Body for the Future

With menopause, I have felt a deep, instinctual need to lift weights and increase my muscle mass. This is not about aesthetics, though I would love to look good. It is about survival and freedom. Strong muscles support our bones and may help prevent osteoporosis. The work we do now is crucial to ensure we can carry our own shopping and climb stairs when we are older. Building a resilient body for the future begins now.

The Crossroads of 60: A Choice Between Contraction and Expansion

As I have navigated my own journey and observed the women around me, I have come to see that entering your sixties presents a profound crossroads. It feels as though two distinct paths emerge. One path can lead to depression and contraction, a feeling that the best years are behind you. I have noticed that some of my older friends have begun to talk excessively, and listening to them can be very taxing. The other path is one of gratitude, vitality, and a renewed sense of curiosity. I have also learned that as we age, certain neural connections can weaken, causing us sometimes to speak without a filter and become more cantankerous or bad-tempered. When I shared this with my friends, we made a pact: we would gently and lovingly alert each other if we noticed this happening, so we could avoid becoming women others find taxing to be around.

Of course, the journey is not a straight line. We may find ourselves straddling both paths, experiencing moments of both sadness and joy. But the ultimate direction we take is a conscious choice. It is the choice between looking back with regret and looking forward with optimism, with support from the friends who have agreed to help us stay on the kindest path.

Clearing the Fog: Reclaiming Your Mind

One of the most universal experiences of menopause is brain fog. I read that one in five women leaves their jobs due to brain fog during menopause. When it happens to me, I do not force it. I simply let it pass. This is not a sign of failure; it is a call for gentleness. It is your brain recalibrating itself. When I cannot recall a word or idea, I let it go, and most of the time, it returns. If I try to force it, my brain does not cooperate. I am learning to live softly, as Tara Styles says.

The Spiritual Awakening: The Wisdom of Letting Go

Beneath the tumult of physical and emotional changes, something else begins to stir. As we grow older, we become calmer and more philosophical. This, for me, has been the greatest gift of this season. We finally stop caring so much about what others think. This is the great spiritual liberation of the Second Spring. I believe that when we heal ourselves, we heal our lineage and all our family. Instead of merely ageing gracefully, we can aim to age powerfully.

This is also a time for discernment. I have seen YouTube videos of women claiming to remove wrinkles by using vaginal cream on their faces. I noticed their skin appeared very unnatural and shiny, so I do not think I will be trying that. Whenever I take a course, I always observe the instructor. If they look well and demonstrate what they preach, I feel inspired to follow them. This is one of the reasons I want to look my best before publishing this book. I need to inspire other women by showing what can be achieved naturally.

Our culture is obsessed with the beauty of youth, but I have come to believe that the most profoundly attractive quality an older woman can possess has nothing to do with chasing the past. It is, instead, the visible radiance of a rich inner world. It is an inner peace that settles into her features, making her a calming presence. It is a sparkling sense of humour, particularly the ability to laugh and make fun of herself, which reveals wisdom and a lightness of being that is magnetic. She is a woman who has learned to live in a state of gratitude and joy, and this positivity makes her naturally flexible and optimistic in the face of life's challenges.

It is the way she looks after her body, not with criticism, but with love and respect for the journey it has taken. She knows that a genuine smile is the finest makeup she will ever own, a direct expression of the light within her. Above all, she is a woman who lives with purpose and enthusiasm, fuelled by an ageless curiosity for life. This is the true beauty of the Second Spring: a radiance that cannot be bought or faked, but can only be earned through a life well-lived.

A Vision for the Future of Menopause

My vision for the future is one in which menopause is reclaimed for what it truly is: a natural and sacred progression of life. In this future, it will be a transition largely free from distressing symptoms, because we will have learned how to nourish and support our bodies in preparation for this powerful shift. It will not be seen as an ending, but as the moment when a woman finally steps into her true wisdom and becomes herself fully. It will be a time to thrive, to harness all the knowledge and experience accumulated throughout our lives, and to inspire others with our grace and power. We will be honoured for our experience, surrounded by the loving families and communities we have created, so that our later years become not a lonely decline, but a joyful celebration of a life well-lived.

A Final Thought

Menopause is not a disease to be cured, but a natural and sacred passage to be honoured. It is the moment when your body, mind, and spirit collectively demand that you turn your attention inward. If we are uncertain what to pursue, we must pursue ourselves by becoming the healthiest, most joyful, most healed, and most present version of ourselves. This is your Second Spring. It is your time to bloom.

As nutrition is my greatest passion, I always ask myself: What else is possible? How can I improve?

Your Wisdom to Go

This week's invitation: Begin to reframe your relationship with menopause by taking these three gentle but powerful actions.

1. **Step Up Your Protein:** For the next three days, make a conscious effort to include a source of clean, healthy protein with every meal, especially breakfast. Notice how it affects your energy levels and cravings.

2. **Pick up a Weight:** You do not need a gym. This week, simply pick up something heavy—a bottle of water or a can of beans—and do ten bicep curls with each arm

while you wait for the kettle to boil. Feel your strength.

3. **Practice Letting Go:** The next time you forget a word or a name, resist the urge to struggle for it. Simply smile, say, "It will come to me," and let it go. Notice the gentleness that arises from this small act of self-compassion.

Your Journal Prompts

An invitation for reflection: Take a few quiet moments to ponder these questions.

1. What is the main story—positive or negative—that you have been told, or have told yourself, about menopause? How does that story make you feel in your body?

2. In what area of your life is your body, mind, or spirit asking you to "step up" right now? What is one small, compassionate action you can take in that area this week?

3. If this season of your life is truly a "Second Spring," what do you want to bloom? What new passions, dreams, or ways of being are waiting to emerge?

Chapter 12

Healing the Roots: Your Inner Child and Generational Wisdom

Have you ever found yourself in the midst of a disagreement, reacting with a level of emotion that feels far greater than the situation warrants? Have you ever felt a surge of insecurity, a fear of being left out, or a wave of shame that seems to appear from nowhere? For years, I experienced these moments and was baffled by them. As a capable, adult woman, I could not understand why, in challenging situations, I would sometimes feel so small, so powerless, so much like a little girl.

What I have come to understand is that, in those moments, it was a little girl who was reacting. My inner child felt frightened, unsafe, and insecure. She felt exactly like the seven-year-old who was dropped off at boarding school by her mother. I can still see my mother walking away, and I can still feel the profound sense of abandonment that washed over me. That feeling, I have realised, is still with me at times. Within each of us lives an inner child—the younger version of ourselves who holds these core memories and emotions. Healing is not about ignoring this child. It is about turning towards her with the love, understanding, and safety she may not have received in the past. This chapter is about learning to heal your roots so you can change the way you grow.

The Invisible Operating System

Our inner child is the keeper of our foundational beliefs and rules about ourselves and the world. These beliefs, formed in our tender years, become the invisible operating system that governs our adult lives.

As a child, I always felt that I did not belong. I was born and loved very much, but my primary companions were my two older brothers and two older cousins, who were not at all impressed that I could not play football. From there, I was sent to a boarding school, where I was terribly homesick. Then, I came to London and felt like an alien. For decades, the core operating belief in my system was, "I do not belong." That belief is perhaps why I left in the first place—to try to find a place where I could finally feel I belonged.

As I write this, I realise that we must look back and honour the resilience it took to reach where we are today. The first step in any healing journey is to gently acknowledge the old operating system. While decoding my subconscious mind, I have learned to communicate with this system. I have created a new version of myself called Lu. I believe we are the creators of our own lives, and our subconscious is our assistant. I have learned not to adopt a victim mentality, because this belief is so empowering. But we must learn its language: it only works in the present tense and does not understand "NO." If we say, "I do not want to eat cake," the subconscious hears, "I want to eat cake!"

The Echoes of the Past: Generational Healing

Our inner child's story is not just her own; it is also woven from the threads of the generations that came before us. The little girl who was afraid of the world was feeling her own fear, but she was also absorbing the fear of her mother, who lived through the Spanish Civil War, and her mother before her. The most influential relationship I have is the one I have with myself, and it is also the most challenging. Being raised in Spain under Franco's dictatorship and the Catholic religion has instilled in me a sense of fear and guilt that I am still trying to shake off in my sixties. We inherit these patterns of fear and grief.

But our generation is here to heal. We are here to break these patterns. This is sacred work. If you are a seeker, it is likely that you, too, are a pattern-breaker. You are here to heal not only your own wounds, but also the echoes of the past that live within you. I believe that when we heal ourselves, we also, in some way, heal the wounds of our ancestors who came before us, and certainly those who will come after us.

The Art of Re-Parenting: Becoming Your Own Loving Adult

The most profound shift in my entire wellness journey happened the moment I truly took ownership of my life. It is the moment you stop seeing life as a series of random events that happen to you, and you start seeing it as a reality that is, in some way, being created by you. This is not about blame; it is about empowerment. When something challenging happens now, I no longer ask, "Why is this happening to me?" Instead, my life has become a beautiful and constant curiosity. I now ask two very different and far more powerful questions: "Why did I create this?" and "What am I supposed to learn from this?" These questions change everything. They take you out of a state of powerless victimhood and place you in the seat of the conscious creator of your experience. They transform every obstacle into an assignment from your soul, every challenge into a lesson, and every difficult person into a teacher. This is the ultimate freedom: to know that you are not just a passenger in your life, but the one who is co-creating the entire journey.

Once we become aware of our inner child and the generational patterns we carry, the most beautiful work can begin: the art of re-parenting. This is the practice of consciously giving yourself the love, validation, and support that your younger self needed.

For me, this has meant a fundamental shift in my internal dialogue. When I make a mistake, I apply the same wisdom I used to give my students: "We do the best we know how. When we know better, we do better." This is the voice of the loving parent I am learning to be for myself. It is a voice of compassion, not criticism. It also takes a physical form. I have been working with my inner child by keeping the only picture I have of myself as a child in my room. I look at it, send her love, and take her out to play when I remember. I forget sometimes that she is there, but when I return to my childhood home, I revert to her and feel insecure and unsafe, just as I did when I was little.

Honouring the Roots: The Mothers and Carers

My relationship with my mother was very intense, full of love and sorrow, because we lived so far apart. Now that I have lost her, I am trying to cope with grief. It is an emotion that comes and goes, invisible until it surfaces when you least expect it. Her last years were hard; her mind was all there, but her body was in pain. I have developed the theory that, in old age, we either lose our minds or our bodies give way.

In her final years, my mum had a wonderful carer named Patricia from Nicaragua. She was an angel, looking after her with a dedication I admired. My mum became so reliant on her that she preferred Patricia to do things for her rather than me, because Patricia knew better. I wish we could all find someone like this in our later years. We must always honour the remarkable people who leave their countries and families to do demanding work so that they can give their children a better future.

This brings me to Fimi, another angel from the Philippines who lived with us for twelve years and helped me care for my children. She was the calmest and most generous human being I have ever encountered. She did everything with a sense of joy and managed to send her three children to university.

A Vision for the Future of Our Roots

My dream for the future of healing is that we will evolve to a place where the deep work of mending our lineage is no longer a burden, but an innate gift we are born with. In this future, we will develop the ability to heal all past generations from the moment we enter this world. Instead of unconsciously carrying the burdens of our ancestors, their fears, their sorrows, their unresolved traumas, we will begin life with a clean slate. This does not mean we will forget the past. Rather, we will be born with the profound ability to learn from it without being defined by it, using the stories of our lineage not as a heavy cloak we are forced to wear, but as a library of wisdom that informs our future and gives us the strength to create a new, more conscious world.

A Final Thought

Healing your roots is not about dwelling in the past. It is about liberating your present and your future. When you connect with and heal your inner child, you are not erasing your history; you are integrating it. The frightened little girl does not disappear; she simply learns that she can finally relax because there is a wise, capable, and loving adult who will always take care of her. This is the journey to wholeness, to becoming the person you were always meant to be. We never fully get there, and that is fine, as we are on a lifelong journey of self-discovery.

Your Wisdom to Go

This week's invitation: Begin the gentle and sacred work of connecting with your inner child with these three simple practices.

1. **Find the Photo:** Locate a photograph of yourself as a small child (ideally between the ages of five and eight). Place it somewhere you will see it every day. For one week, simply look at it each morning with kindness and send that child love.

2. **Ask, "What Do You Need?":** The next time you feel an overwhelming emotional reaction, pause for a moment. Place a hand on your heart and gently ask the younger part of you, "What do you need right now?" Listen for the answer.

3. **Schedule a Playdate:** Look at your calendar and schedule a thirty-minute "playdate" with your inner child this week. This should be an activity with no

goal other than pure, simple fun, such as colouring, dancing to an old song, or eating your favourite childhood treat.

Your Journal Prompts

An invitation for reflection: Take a few quiet moments to ponder these questions.

1. What is the primary emotional "weather" you remember from your childhood home (e.g., joyful, tense, quiet, chaotic)? How does that weather still show up in your life today?

2. What is one core belief about yourself (e.g., "I must not make mistakes," "I am too much") that you know was formed when you were very young?

3. If you could go back in time and give your eight-year-old self a single message, what would it be? Write it down as a letter to her.

Conclusion

The Way Forward – Creating a New Paradigm

I have come to realise that my twenty-year journey of wellness has distilled itself into the lifelong practice of asking three fundamental questions. These are the inquiries I return to day after day, and they form the very heart of the way forward. The first is, "How do I keep myself healthy and fit?", a question that honours the body as the sacred vehicle for this life. The second is, "How do I relate with people I disagree with from a place of love?", a question that calls for compassion and recognises that we are all one. The third and most profound question is, "How do I have a closer relationship with myself and with the presence within me that births the vision of my life?" This final question is the key to our inner world, the source from which all true wellness and joy ultimately flow.

The way forward, as I see it, is not a grand or complicated plan. It is a simple, daily choice. It is the decision to rise each morning, to give thanks for being alive, and to set out to be joyous and kind to ourselves and others. The way forward is a life filled with wellness, not because we are fortunate, but because we learn to seek it and bring it into our lives with intention.

In the new paradigm I love to imagine, we would spend our lives pursuing our passions, using our creativity to make this world a better place. A world without wars, those pointless conflicts that just thinking about breaks my heart. Why do humans never seem to learn? Perhaps if more women ruled the world, we would have greater peace. Perhaps. To create a better world, we must first have the courage to imagine it.

The Power of One: Navigating a Troubled World

It is easy to feel overwhelmed by the state of the world. The weight of its problems can feel crushing to the spirit. I have learned that just because one feels everything, it does not mean one is responsible for everything. I have had to learn to focus on love and compassion; otherwise, I would be consumed by despair. We are living in unprecedented times, and many feel hopeless and disillusioned. It is time for hope and inspiration.

The way forward is not paved with cynicism but with love, joy, and optimism. I have a deep and abiding faith in the resilience of human beings. We are incredibly resourceful and creative. We are at a moment when we can wake up and decide to co-create a better world, a society not driven by money, but by the desire to make this earth the paradise it could be.

Building a New Paradigm: A Vision for the Future

This new world requires us to rethink the very systems that structure our lives.

Our education system must change radically. It is a relic of the industrial age in the digital era we are entering, no longer fit for purpose. The pressure of exams, the fear of failure, these are not conducive to true learning. I imagine a future where education is a joyful, lifelong experience, where individuals are free to pursue their own interests and passions.

Our workplaces will also have to change. They should be places of cooperation, where teams work together for a common goal, not battlefields where individuals compete. I believe workers should be shareholders in the businesses they help to build.

Politicians and the entire political system must change so that only people committed to real transformation can access a system that should be transparent, free from corruption, and based on co-operation. Politicians should have genuine credentials to demonstrate they possess the experience and wisdom to lead the country and the economy, and to make sound decisions for the good of society.

And we, as individuals, must change. We need to stop the endless accumulation of things and simplify our lives. Instead of spending our lives working at jobs we dislike to buy things we do not need, to impress people we do not like, we can choose to spend our time doing what we love and accumulating magical moments. A magical moment is the sound of my granddaughter's voice when she calls me "Yaya." It is the feeling of sitting under a canopy of Sakura trees in Japan. These are the moments that weave the tapestry of a rich and beautiful life.

Dreaming is free, and I dream of a world where: no one goes hungry or is homeless, there are no wars, the sick are healed, no child is an orphan, animals are treated with respect, we care for the planet, we stop buying things we do not need, and people co-operate and care for each other for the greater good. And if most of us want this, why is it not happening?

Creating Your Own Way Forward: A Modern Vision

My personal way forward, like everyone else's, is uncertain. But through a programme called Lifebook, and with the help of modern tools, I have created a vision of what my life can be like in five years. I have embraced Artificial Intelligence, which is here to stay. It has helped co-create a possible life vision even better than what I could have imagined on my own. I want to share part of that vision with you, not as a prescription, but as an example of what is possible when you live with clarity and intention.

My Life Vision Statement

As I sit in my beautifully designed London home, my sanctuary, I feel a profound sense of alignment and purpose. At 67, I have transformed into the most vibrant, powerful, and authentic version of myself—a beacon of inspiration.

My health is a testament to my commitment to wellness. My body is a vision of vitality, free from chronic conditions and reliance on medication. It is nourished by the vibrant, warming foods I love—a joyful blend of Mediterranean and Chinese wisdom. Much of what I eat comes from my own garden, where I cultivate not just vegetables, but a deep connection to nature. My daily routine seamlessly blends intentional movement, spiritual practices, and joyful walks. I move with the grace of a tiger—my Chinese zodiac sign. My 165cm frame is lean, muscular, and strong. I am not just ageing gracefully; I am ageing powerfully, mastering the art of growing younger from the inside out and proving that age is truly just a number.

With my husband, my greatest teacher, I have cultivated a partnership of deep peace, mutual respect, and unconditional love. We have learned to be a team, supporting each other's individual passions while creating a shared life filled with laughter, travel, and quiet companionship. Our home is a sanctuary, not just for us, but because of us—a testament to a love that has weathered life's storms and emerged stronger, calmer, and more profound than ever.

My relationships are my most precious treasure. With my children and granddaughter, I share a bond of unconditional love and mutual respect. We support each other's dreams and create magical moments. My life is also woven into a rich tapestry of friendship, including the deep, conscious connections of my virtual accountability groups, who mirror my growth and hold me to my highest self.

Spiritually, I am deeply connected. Meditation, astrology, and continuous self-improvement are not just practices, but a way of life. My inner peace is unshakeable.

My life is filled with purpose, creativity, and the freedom to travel the world with ease and joy. As a Generator in Human Design, I have learned to respond to life's opportunities with authenticity and excitement. My vision is not just about personal achievement, but about creating a ripple effect of positive transformation. Through my book and my way of being, I inspire millions of women to see what can be achieved naturally, empowering them to embrace their own journey of holistic wellness and authentic living.

The Final Frontier: Healing the Relationship with Yourself

The greatest work we will all do, the true way forward, is healing our relationship with our true self and our spirit. This is ongoing work that is never fully completed, unlike most things in life.

This brings me to a final question. When we are 99 years old and sitting in a rocking chair, where do we want to be? Who do we want to be surrounded by? And most importantly, how do we want to feel? The way forward begins the moment we decide to live our way into those answers.

155

Epilogue

100 Truths for a Life Well Lived

After a lifetime of seeking, learning, and growing, what remains are the simple yet powerful truths. The journey of wellness is not about accumulating complex knowledge, but about returning to the fundamental wisdom that resides within us all. It is the kind of wisdom I imagine a wise 100-year-old might share from her rocking chair, earned through a life of love and lessons.

This final chapter is a gift from my heart to yours. It is a collection of one hundred pieces of advice, lessons learned through joy and sorrow, success and failure. These are not rules to be followed, but signposts for your own journey. May you return to them whenever you need a guiding light on your path.

On Your Relationship with Yourself

1. The most important relationship you will ever have is the one you have with yourself.
2. Stop worrying about what others think and concentrate on what you think.
3. You regret what you do not do, not what you do.

4. Forgive others and yourself, always.

5. Talk to yourself as if you were your best friend.

6. Accept yourself as you are, but strive to be the best version of yourself.

7. Do not live so much in your head; listen to your body more.

8. Spend time observing your thoughts; they are not you.

9. Do not give your power to others.

10. Boundaries help people understand how you want to be treated.

11. No matter what others think, always believe in yourself.

12. Your subconscious mind is there for you; it is your assistant.

13. Honour yourself by valuing your greatness.

14. When we learn to say NO to others, we say YES to ourselves.

15. Our mind is like a radio station; tune into what you want to listen to.

16. Ask yourself: What do I want? What do I need? What is enough?

17. Thoughts are not facts.

18. Aim for self-actualisation, to become more and more of who you truly are.

19. Do not allow yourself to be formatted and conditioned.

On Health, Joy, and Well-being

20. Look after your body; it is your vehicle for this life.

21. Do not save money on food; always buy the best quality you can afford.

22. The body can heal itself.

23. Feel all your emotions and talk about how you feel.

24. When you suppress your emotions, you suppress your immune system.

25. The purpose of your relationship with your body is to listen to it and treasure it.

26. We are constantly seeking comfort from discomfort. Observe your discomfort.

27. Happiness is not the aim; it is the path.

28. Be grateful; many people did not wake up today.

29. Make yourself happy.

30. Your bed and your sofa should be the most comfortable things in your home.

31. Grow things that make you happy, such as flowers and food you can eat.

32. Guilt is a painful companion of grief.

33. Grief is silent and invisible, so when it comes, let it be.

34. Use your body to tell you what it needs.

35. Your brain, like your body, needs to be exercised.

On Navigating Life and the World

36. In the end, it all works out.

37. Everything happens for a reason.

38. Ninety per cent of the things you worry about do not happen. The others do.

39. Live in the moment. Yesterday is gone, tomorrow never comes, but the present is a present.

40. Do not rush; there is plenty of time to do all that truly matters.

41. Learn lessons quickly so you do not have to keep repeating them.

42. Go with the flow.

43. The hardest times are the ones that help you grow the most.

44. Do not regret the past; look forward.

45. Difficult situations are opportunities to grow and learn.

46. There are no problems, only situations to resolve.

47. If you are not sure, do not do it.

48. Dreams are not supposed to be realistic.

49. Life is a film; you are the main character and the producer. Make a good film.

50. We all do the best we know how. When we know better, we do better.

51. Do not let addictions control your life, or you will lose your freedom.

52. Rushing is like taking money from your bank account. Rich people do not rush.

53. When confronted with a challenge, ask yourself: What if it were easier?

54. Life is now, and the best time is now.

55. Life is simple, easy, and fun.

On Connection, Love, and Relationships

56. We are all one.

57. Have friends of different ages and from different walks of life.

58. Your children do not do what you tell them to do; they do what they see you do.

59. Your partner in life will teach you your biggest lessons.

60. People do not remember what you say, but they always remember how you made them feel.

61. We are mirrors of each other. Discover what you dislike in others that you also possess but cannot see.

62. Do not waste your time with people who are energy vampires.

63. Give people a second chance; we all make mistakes.

64. Toxic relationships not only drain us but also prevent us from developing new relationships.

65. Wise people talk about issues, not about other people.

66. We are not here to solve other people's problems, only to share time with them.

67. When someone speaks about something we do not agree with, we can say: I know this is your belief, and I respect it. I do not want to talk about it for my own well-being.

68. Help others whenever you can.

69. Do not try to change others.

70. Choose carefully who you share things with. Will they be happy for you?

On a Life of Purpose and Meaning

71. Shine and inspire others.

72. Follow your heart.

73. Do not spend your life doing a job you hate, as it will destroy your soul.

74. Live a comfortable life. You are here to enjoy, not to suffer unnecessarily.

75. Accumulate magical moments, not things.

76. Travel light, as possessions can weigh you down.

77. Be clear about what you want so that you can manifest it.

78. Live as if you are going to live forever and as if you are going to die tomorrow.

79. Travel as much as you can, as it enriches your life in ways you may not even realise.

80. Do not share your plans.

81. Always have dreams and aspirations.

82. Every day, try to make your life and the lives of others better.

83. Share your learnings.

84. Love wealth and money, so they come to you, and you can share them.

85. Pay your bills with joy; money is meant to circulate, not stagnate.

86. Do not cling to or attach yourself to things or people.

87. Never lose hope.

88. Average people want to keep you average.

89. You have more than enough, and you can give it away because you know how to create it.

90. Have a list of things to stop doing.

91. Be open to receiving more good than you have ever experienced or wished for.

92. Learn from nature.

93. Your greatest commodity is your time; spend it as you choose.

94. To think more clearly, embrace the silence of meditation.

95. We are powerful manifestors.

96. To understand the world, read. To understand yourself, write.

97. When we come together, we create more possibilities for growth and transformation.

98. Simplify your life; we do not need eighty per cent of what we own.

99. When we need to feel safe, our judgment takes over, and what we need to do is ask for guidance.

100. It is up to us to decide how we approach the choices in life. We are more likely to regret what we have not done than what we have.

Appendix A

A Toolkit of Quick and Easy Remedies

Wellness does not always require grand gestures. Sometimes, the most profound shifts come from the small, simple remedies we can turn to in our daily lives. This list is a collection of my most trusted, go-to practices. Think of this as your quick-reference toolkit.

- **For Minor Burns:** Apply a drop of lavender oil directly to the area.

- **For Digestion & Heartburn:** Gently boil a tablespoon each **of cumin, coriander, fennel,** and fenugreek seeds in water for a few minutes. Strain and drink the warm tea.

- **For Morning Hydration:** Start your day with a glass of warm water, lemon, and Celtic salt to help hydrate and cleanse the body.

- **For Reducing Wrinkles:** Gently massage a blend of castor oil with jojoba and frankincense oil onto your face.

- **To Promote Sleep:** Lightly spray magnesium oil or eucalyptus oil on the soles of your feet before bed.

- **For Gut Health & Collagen: Bone broth** is one of the best and most absorbable ways to boost collagen and heal the gut.

- **For Nourishment & Hydration: Juices and smoothies** are a simple way to increase your intake of vegetables, fruits, and fibre.

- **To Shift Your Energy: Dancing** is one of the fastest ways to shift a heavy feeling.

- **To Grow Eyebrows:** A folk remedy that seems to be working for me is applying castor oil mixed with a little onion juice.

- **For Sore Throats:** Applying iodine to the skin on your neck may help it heal faster.

- **For a Fever or Cold:** Remember the old wisdom: "Starve a fever and feed a cold."

- **Parasite cleanse:** 1 teaspoon of organic cold-pressed oil, organic raw honey, cayenne pepper, fresh garlic, fresh lemon and crushed cloves. Take every morning for three weeks and rest one week. Do it for three months.

- **The Ultimate Health Remedy:** The best way to improve gut health and health in general is to reduce stress.

Appendix B

An Invitation to Live with Intention

The journey of wellness is a journey of intention. It is about consciously choosing how we want to live, feel, and show up in the world each day. As a final thought, I wanted to share my own personal aims—the intentions I am setting for the years I have left on this beautiful planet. This list is not a prescription, but an invitation. I share it with you as an open-hearted example, in the hope that it might inspire you to create your own.

My Aims for a Life of Wellness:

- Live in peace and harmony
- Help and inspire
- Reverse ageing
- Listen to my body and my soul
- Create magical moments
- Live in joy and be grateful all the time
- Seize opportunities
- Be love and light
- Keep centred and be in alignment
- Spend time in nature

- Be kind to myself
- Continue to be in love with life
- Spend magical time with my granddaughter
- Never stop playing
- Learn something new every day
- Do random acts of kindness
- Pass on my wisdom to those who will listen
- Perfect the act of living
- Forgive everyone, starting with myself
- Feel that I matter and make a difference by being here
- Remember I am unique and special, like all of us are
- Be my authentic self
- Continue to feel that we are all one
- Travel as much as I can
- Endeavour to know and understand myself better every day
- Observe and redirect my thoughts
- Develop my spiritual life
- Use your gifts to the benefit of others
- Try new things and experiences
- Learn to digest life so that I can digest my food better
- Improve the world with intentions and actions
- Live softly without rushing or stressing

- Maintain my enthusiasm for life

- Gain new insights

- Become less gullible without becoming close-minded

- Be patient with myself and others

- Never lose hope for better things to come

- Have faith in the new generations

- Be able to see the darkness in the world without becoming sad

- Know that we can have conflicting views and coexist

- Do not waste energy arguing with other people

- Learn to do nothing and be bored

- Work on feeling good inside

- Have more presence

- Flow through life

- Appreciate all forms of art

- Continue to work on chewing my food consciously

- Reduce stomach fat and build lean muscle in my body

- Work on body strength so I can open a jar when I am older

- Have a good morning routine

Bibliography

Your Continuing Wellness Library

The journey of wellness is a lifelong adventure of learning and discovery. No single book holds all the answers, but every author and every story can be a wonderful teacher. The books listed here have been my companions, guides, and sources of inspiration over my twenty-year quest. They have challenged my thinking, deepened my understanding, and illuminated my path.

I share them with you not as a required reading list, but as an open-hearted invitation to continue your own journey. May you find in these pages the same wisdom, comfort, and inspiration that they have so generously given me.

- **Berger, Anna,** "Escape Your Matrix"
- **Brooks, Arthur C. and Oprah Winfrey,** "Build the life you want."
- **Brown, Brené,** "The Gifts of Imperfection" or "Daring Greatly"
- **Chapman, Gary,** "The 5 Love Languages"
- **Chödrön, Pema,** "When Things Fall Apart: Heart Advice for Difficult Times"

- **Chopra, Deepak,** "The Seven Spiritual Laws of Success"
- **Clear, James,** "Atomic Habits"
- **Coelho, Paulo,** "The Alchemist"
- **Conley, Chip,** "Learning to love midlife"
- **Covey, Stephen R.,** "The 7 Habits of Highly Effective People"
- **Diamond, Marie,** "Feng Shui your Life"
- **Dispenza, Dr Joe,** "Meditations for Breaking the Habit of Being You"
- **Doidge, Dr Norman,** "The Brain That Changes Itself"
- **Doyle, Laura,** "The Empowered Wife"
- **Dyer, Dr Wayne,** "Change Your Thoughts, Change Your Mind"
- **Frankl, Viktor E.,** "Man's Search for Meaning"
- **Garcia, Hector and Francesc Miralles,** "Ikigai"
- **Gundry, Dr Steven R.,** "The Plant Paradox"
- **Hays, Louise,** "You Can Heal Your Life"
- **Hendricks, Gay,** "The Big Leap"
- **Hicks, Esther and Jerry,** "Ask and It Is Given"
- **Hill, Napoleon,** "Think and Be Rich"
- **Holford, Patrick,** "The Optimum Nutrition Bible"
- **Hyman, Dr Mark,** "Young Forever"

- **Iriarte, Diana López,** "Despierta la energía que hay dentro de ti (Awaken the energy you have inside)"
- **Katie, Byron,** "Loving What Is: Four Questions That Can Change Your Life"
- **Kern Lima, Jamie,** "Worthy"
- **King, Vex,** "Healing is the New High"
- **Li, Dr William,** "Eat to Beat the Diet"
- **Lipton, Bruce,** "The Biology of Belief"
- **McCarey, Dr Gladys,** "The Well-Lived Life"
- **Megre, Vladimir,** "Anastasia"
- **Morter, Dr Sue,** "The Energy Codes"
- **Myss, Caroline,** "Anatomy of the Spirit"
- **Northrup, Dr Christiane,** "The Wisdom of Menopause"
- **O'Neill, Barbara,** "Sustain me"
- **Pollan, Michael,** "In Defence of Food: An Eater's Manifesto"
- **Robins, Mel,** "The 5 Second Rule"
- **Romm, Dr Aviva,** "Hormone Intelligence"
- **Ruiz, Don Miguel,** "The Four Agreements"
- **Schucman, Helen,** "A Course in Miracles"
- **Shefali, Dr,** "A Radical Awakening"
- **Shetty, Jay,** "Think Like a Monk"

- **Singer, Michael A.,** "The Untethered Soul"

- **Spector, Tim,** "The Diet Myth"

- **Tolle, Eckhart,** "A New Earth"

- **Vitti, Alisa,** "In the FLO: Unlock Your Hormonal Advantage and Revolutionise Your Life"

- **Weil, Dr Andrew,** "Spontaneous Healing"

- **William, Anthony,** "Liver Rescue"

- **Wolynn, Mark,** "It Didn't Start with You"

- **Wren, Barbara,** "Cellular Awakening"